THE Soul's AWAKENING

SOUL AND SPIRITUAL EVENTS IN DRAMATIC SCENES

RUDOLF STEINER

TEMPLE LODGE
London

Translated by Michael Hedley Burton and Adrian Locher

Temple Lodge Publishing
51 Queen Caroline Street
London W6 9QL

Published by Temple Lodge 1994

This book is a translation of *Der Seelen Erwachen*, published as part of *Vier Mysteriendramen* (volume 14 in the *Rudolf Steiner Gesamtausgabe* or Collected Works) by Rudolf Steiner Verlag, Dornach

© Temple Lodge Publishing 1994
This translation © Portal Productions 1994

Where appropriate, the moral right of the author has been asserted under the Copyright, Designs and Patents Act, 1988

All rights reserved. No part of this publication may be reproduced, stored in a retrieval system, or transmitted, in any form or by any means, electronic, mechanical, photocopying, recording or otherwise, without the prior permission of the publishers

A catalogue record for this book is available from the British Library

ISBN 0 904693 65 1

Cover by Charlene Collison and Ivon Oates
Typeset by DP Photosetting, Aylesbury, Bucks
Printed and bound in Great Britain by Cromwell Press Limited, Broughton Gifford, Wiltshire

TRANSLATOR'S PREFACE

This translation of *The Soul's Awakening* was created for Portal Productions' international tour of the drama in 1994/95. It therefore came about to meet the needs of a particular production by a particular group of English-speaking performing artists. This group began performing Steiner's cycle of four mystery dramas in 1989 with the first, *The Portal of Initiation*. For this production one of the three already existing translations was naturally used. But as the work evolved, and the second and third dramas—*The Challenge of the Soul* and *The Guardian of the Threshold*—were performed in 1991 and 1992 respectively to ever wider audiences, there was an increasing need for a translation more attuned to the ears of English-speaking actors and audiences today. The text for the third drama was a mixture of previous translations and actors' interpretations. But in 1993, in preparation for the fourth drama, *The Soul's Awakening*, the group decided to undertake an entirely new translation.

This translation was originally intended to be an actor's text—a text, that is, which was to be put through the process of the rehearsal period, in which alterations would certainly have been made. This will no doubt still be the case for the final spoken version of the performance. But the advantages of having a published text of the translation at the time of the performances outweighed the original idea of waiting for the final version before we went to print. And so, like the production itself, which exists in time and could never be done exactly the same way at another time, with a different cast and director, may this translation be seen for what it is—work in progress.

Our thanks are due to the previous translators—Harry Collison, Ruth and Hans Pusch, and Adam Bittleston—whose translations were always close at hand (and a few of whose lines finally proved irresistible!). Without their work our task would have been so much more difficult. We would also like to express our gratitude to Johanna Collis for her generous professional help with specific questions on German meaning. And lastly, we would like to thank our friends and colleagues in Portal Productions for entrusting us with this awesome and wonderful task.

Michael Burton
Adrian Locher

July 1994

INTRODUCTION

Rudolf Steiner's mystery dramas, written between 1909 and 1913, deal with the spiritual mysteries of human life. They have very little to do with the different cycles of medieval mystery plays or the detective mysteries we know today, except that in all three the word 'mystery' indicates something that is not known or understood.

From the seven dramas that were planned Steiner only completed the tetralogy of four, which show us a style of theatre that diverges radically in form and content from anything that hitherto has been written in the genre of theatre. They address issues generally seen as taboo because they depict events, feelings and thoughts that lie beyond our normal consciousness and can only be perceived by someone who has achieved a high stage of initiation, that is to say, is able to consciously look into the happenings of the supersensible world.

The dramas deal with three major themes: the path of self-development leading to initiation; an understanding of the opposing forces trying to hinder this; and learning the laws of reincarnation and karma as a precondition for attaining self-knowledge, understanding relationships, and community building.

Drama, as all art, is an experience of a threshold, unifying the world of matter with the world of spirit through the soul of the artist. The greater the inner experience of the artist, the more work it takes to forge it into matter. The complexity of the spiritual world is so great and our concepts so limited, inasmuch as they are predominantly derived from the world of matter, that it demands a master of wordsmithing to be able to find a form (language) that is in harmony with the content (spirit).

Rudolf Steiner has, in expressing his experiences of the spiritual world in the form of dramas, created a living artistic threshold that must be continually recreated according to the demands of the time. Thus the play moves and develops, creating a revelation of the spirit that is far closer to its essence, namely, metamorphosis and change. In order to manifest this, Steiner has created new words and word combinations as well as finding an onomatopoeic sensitivity in which certain indescribable experiences are made audible through using different combinations of sounds, so that the meaning is *experienced* rather than understood. He has also used a style whose verbal tapestry consists of the subtext. That is to say, the characters continually verbalize their innermost thoughts and feelings. There is, therefore, no discrepancy between word and deed, inner and outer—that which forms the very lifeblood of a normal play! The dramatic tension here lies in the juxtaposition of events within the stream of destiny as it is experienced from the other side of the threshold, above and beyond the everyday consciousness.

Rudolf Steiner's mystery dramas are essentially dramas of the spoken word. Although any play can in theory be performed within any theatre tradition or method, the form of these dramas demands a different style of theatrecraft than has hitherto been available. One that has developed out of spiritual investigation, or Anthroposophy, attempts to imbue the whole human being with the word, so that the word is not only heard, but *seen*. This approach aims to encompass, yet transcend, our senses, intellect and emotions, bringing about an inner experience that elevates theatre to an act of communion between the artists and the audience. Performed in this way, these modern mystery dramas can inspire a new theatre culture, a new theatre of the word.

Christopher Marcus (Director of Portal Productions' production of The Soul's Awakening)

London, July 1994

RESUME OF THE FIRST THREE DRAMAS

Rudolf Steiner's cycle of mystery dramas portrays a group of people who are consciously undergoing a path of spiritual development. As the cycle unfolds, it becomes apparent that this particular group has also been together in former lives on earth at certain critical turning points in the evolution of humanity. In the second drama, we see them in medieval times, involved in the historical conflicts surrounding the Church's suppression of the Knights Templar Order. The fourth drama shows them working together in the initiation rituals of a temple in ancient Egypt. And throughout the cycle of dramas, we follow them in their present lives, when they are united again as pupils of a modern spiritual teaching.

Their spiritual teacher, **Benedictus**, guides them in such a way that they have complete freedom—and they make many mistakes along the way—but he always acts out of a responsibility he carries for the destiny of his pupils. The group consists of seven main characters: **Johannes Thomasius**, whom we meet at first as a young painter; his friend **Maria**, an older woman who is the most advanced pupil of Benedictus; **Professor Capesius**, a respected historian; his friend **Dr Strader**, a scientist; **Theodora**, a younger woman who has the gift of seership; **Felix Balde**, a mystic imbued with nature-wisdom; and **Felicia Balde**, his wife, the teller of magical fairy-tales.

As these characters advance in self-knowledge, they encounter various powers working in the world and in the human soul, which either help or hinder their development. These powers are portrayed in the dramas as supersensible beings. **Lucifer** ('the Lord of Wishes') is the power which through beauty and art lifts the soul beyond the limitations of earthly life, but at the same time can inflate the self through pride and bring about a shirking of earthly responsibility. **Ahriman** ('the Father of Deceit') is the power which makes possible objective scientific thinking but at the same time works to conceal all traces of humanity's connection to the spiritual world. **The Guardian of the Threshold** is the spiritual being who protects the spiritual world from the harmful influences resulting from human beings entering it before they have developed themselves sufficiently. Unconscious elements of the soul are objectified and shown as definite supersensible entities: the shadow, or **'Double' of Johannes Thomasius**; the **Spirit of Johannes' Youth**. Then there are revealed different powers of the human soul which are working to help it unite with the spiritual world—**Philia, Astrid** and **Luna**—and the power that works to preserve the more earthly human personality—**the Other Philia**.

Much of the drama of **Johannes** revolves around his relationship to Maria. When they first met, she quickly became his spiritual mentor and the inspirer of his art. In the first drama, we see how this results in Johannes having to come face to face with the experience of his own worthlessness. But, through the guidance of Benedictus and through his love for Maria, he is able to overcome this and to take great steps in his own spiritual development. In the second drama, we find Johannes relying too heavily on Maria for his spiritual and artistic work. It is shown that this is a consequence of their relationship in medieval times. At that time, Johannes was a miner called Thomas, employed by Knights of the Templar Order. Maria was a monk who shaped his mind and made him turn against these Knights, one of whom was his own long-lost father (an earlier incarnation of Capesius). In becoming aware of this, Maria realizes she must separate from Johannes in order that he can develop out of his own strength. But Johannes is shattered by this separation, which forces him to recognize and confront his own weaknesses. He changes his direction in life, gives up painting and writes a book about spiritual knowledge.

However, whilst he is emphasizing this more logical, intellectual side of his nature, he unwittingly allows powers of desire and compulsion to grow in secret in his own unconscious depths. Much of the action of the third drama is concerned with what results from this. Lucifer is able to foster and inflame an illicit desire in Johannes towards Theodora, who is, by this time, married to Dr Strader. This power in his attraction to her works into Theodora's life so strongly that she is drained of strength and dies. Maria, still united to Johannes in spirit, stands against the power of Lucifer, making a 'sacred vow' to renounce all feeling of enjoyment and satisfaction that normally results from the development of one's own inner powers.

Through the healing force working in this vow, Johannes is led to see himself and master his desires, but he is left in a difficult, somewhat split state of being. He has been assisted by Benedictus and Maria to develop higher clairvoyant powers, but these can only work rightly when he keeps them strictly guarded from the concerns and wishes of his normal, conscious self. He vows to do this, but it is a temporary situation only and, from the first time we see him in the fourth drama, the dilemma of his divided personality is demanding attention. The fourth drama has as a main theme the attempt of Johannes to make peace between his higher and lower selves.

When we first meet **Capesius**, he is new to the teachings of Benedictus, and stands on the outside of the group. During the course of the first drama, we see him grappling with the new and revolutionary way of thinking presented by Benedictus, and thereby entering into closer relationship with the other pupils. To begin with, he can approach the spiritual world more readily through listening to the fairy-tales of Felicia Balde, and these restore him at times when his own forces are depleted. In the second drama, he breaks through to his own spiritual perceptions and has a vision of his life in medieval times. He learns that at that time he deserted his wife and his two children to join the order of the Knights Templar. His wife died, and the children, Thomas and Celia, grew up separately. (These children are the previous incarnations of Johannes and Theodora.) Celia was brought up by foster parents (the previous incarnations of Felix and Felicia Balde). Thomas and Celia are later reunited and fall in love, not realizing that they are brother and sister. When this is discovered, their planned marriage cannot go ahead, and it is this unresolved love which Lucifer manipulates in their present lives in the circumstances leading up to the death of Theodora.

Capesius is overwhelmed when he confronts his failure as husband and parent in that life, and becomes unable to deal with the consequences. He seeks refuge in self-forgetfulness in the realm of Lucifer. In the third drama, Maria, Benedictus and Felicia Balde help him to renew his strength and take up full responsibility for his deeds—but he continues to carry in his soul the tendency to turn away from the pain and difficulties of earthly life. This inclination towards other-worldliness, in which Lucifer is working, demands a solution during the course of the fourth drama.

As a modern scientist, **Dr Strader** is, to begin with, the most sceptical of all the characters about the teachings of Benedictus. Yet, through his scientific training, he has developed qualities of objectivity and integrity which make him immune to the temptations Johannes and Capesius fall prey to. Gradually, he develops an awareness of the spiritual world which he is able to apply in his scientific work. In medieval times he was a Jewish healer, an outsider hated by the Church and the peasants in the area where he lived. He found refuge from their persecution behind the walls of the same order of Knights to which Capesius had once belonged. In his spiritual pupilship in this present life, Strader is profoundly helped by Theodora, whom he marries. Assisted by her, Strader takes up the task of developing a machine that makes use of a revolutionary new source of power, and which, if it can be constructed, will greatly affect many aspects of human life. In his research, he penetrates into the realm of Ahriman, and in the third drama we see him confronting this power and learning about its true nature. Strader's invention fails, and the happiness of his marriage is ended after seven years by Theodora's death. As the fourth drama begins, Strader is undertaking a new task as technical adviser in a project sponsored by the owner of a factory, **Hilary Gottgetreu**.

Hilary must be mentioned in connection with three other characters of the earlier dramas—**Romanus, Torquatus** and **Bellicosus**. In the third drama, these characters are shown to be members of a certain Rosicrucian brotherhood, working out of a traditional spirituality active at the beginning of this century. At the end of the third drama, they are superseded in their office by Johannes, Capesius and Strader. This is an important factor underlying the fourth drama; the three pupils of Benedictus carry their spiritual responsibilities in a new way, united with their daily life and practical work in the world. This brings them into conflict with others who continue to work in the old ways, in which spiritual activity and practical life are kept strictly separate. The fourth drama opens as, for the first time, the pupils of Benedictus, invited by Hilary to renew the work of his family business, begin to attempt to make their ideals become reality.

M.B., A.L.

CHARACTERS, FIGURES AND EVENTS

The soul and spiritual events portrayed in *The Soul's Awakening* take place about one year later than those in the preceding play, *The Guardian of the Threshold*.

I THE BEARERS OF THE SPIRITUAL ELEMENT:
1. **Benedictus**: The personality considered by a number of his students to be the knower of profound spiritual relationships. In the preceding soul-portrayals, *The Portal of Initiation* and *The Challenge of the Soul*, he is represented as the leader of the Sun Temple. In *The Guardian of the Threshold*, there is expressed in him that spiritual current which wishes to replace traditional spiritual life, protected by the mystic brotherhood, by a modern, living spirituality. In *The Soul's Awakening*, Benedictus should not be considered as merely standing above his pupils but as interwoven with his own soul destiny in their inner experiences.
2. **Hilary Gottgetreu**: The knower of a traditional spiritual life that is connected with his own spiritual experiences. He is the same individuality who appears in *The Challenge of the Soul* as the Grand Master of a medieval occult brotherhood.
3. **The Business Manager of Hilary Gottgetreu.**
4. **The Secretary of Hilary Gottgetreu**: The same personality as Friedrich Geist in *The Guardian of the Threshold*.

II THE BEARERS OF THE ELEMENT OF DEVOTION:
1. **Magnus Bellicosus**: Called Germanus in *The Portal of Initiation*. In *The Challenge of the Soul*, the same individuality appears as the Second Preceptor of the medieval occult brotherhood.
2. **Albert Torquatus**: Called Theodosius in *The Portal of Initiation*. In *The Challenge of the Soul*, the same individuality appears as the First Master of Ceremonies of the medieval occult brotherhood.
3. **Professor Capesius**: His individuality appears in *The*

Challenge of the Soul as the First Preceptor of the medieval occult brotherhood.
4. **Felix Balde**: In *The Portal of Initiation*, he is the bearer of a certain nature-mysticism; here in *The Soul's Awakening* he is the bearer of subjective mysticism. His individuality appears as Joseph Kean in *The Challenge of the Soul*.

III THE BEARERS OF THE ELEMENT OF WILL:
1. **Romanus**: Here he is reintroduced under the name used for him in *The Portal of Initiation*; this is in accordance with the core of his being which he has been endeavouring to reach in the years lying between the first and fourth play. Friedrich Trautmann is his name in the physical world, used when his inner life has very little to do with the occurring events. His individuality appears in *The Challenge of the Soul* as Second Master of Ceremonies of the medieval occult brotherhood.
2. **Dr Strader**: His individuality appears in *The Challenge of the Soul* as Simon, the Jew.
3. **The Nurse of Dr Strader**: The same personality as Maria Treufels in *The Guardian of the Threshold*. In *The Portal of Initiation* she is known as the Other Maria because the imaginative cognition of Johannes Thomasius forms the picture of certain powers of Nature in her image. Her individuality appears as Bertha, Kean's daughter in *The Challenge of the Soul*.
4. **Felicia Balde**: Her individuality appears in *The Challenge of the Soul* as Dame Kean.

IV THE BEARERS OF THE ELEMENT OF SOUL:
1. **Maria**: Her individuality appears in *The Challenge of the Soul* as the Monk.
2. **Johannes Thomasius**: His individuality appears in *The Challenge of the Soul* as Thomas.
3. **The Wife of Hilary Gottgetreu**.

V BEINGS OF THE SPIRITUAL WORLD:
1. **Lucifer**.
2. **Ahriman**.

3. **Gnomes.**
4. **Sylphs.**

VI BEINGS OF THE HUMAN SPIRITUAL ELEMENT:
1. **Philia.** ⎫ The spiritual beings who further the
2. **Astrid.** ⎬ uniting of human powers of soul with
3. **Luna.** ⎭ the cosmos.
4. **The Other Philia**: The bearer of the element of love in that world to which the spiritual personality belongs.
5. **Theodora's Soul**: Her individuality appears in *The Challenge of the Soul* as Celia, the foster daughter of Kean and sister of Thomas.
6. **The Guardian of the Threshold.**
7. **The Double of Johannes Thomasius.**
8. **Ferdinand Reinecke's Soul** (in Ahriman's realm, Scene 12): He appears as Ferdinand Reinecke only in *The Guardian of the Threshold*.
9. **The Spirit of Johannes' Youth.**

VII

The personalities of Benedictus and Maria also appear as thought-forms—in Scene 2 as those of Johannes Thomasius and in Scene 3 as those of Strader. In Scene 10 Maria appears as the thought-form of Johannes Thomasius.

VIII

The individualities of Benedictus, Hilary Gottgetreu, Magnus Bellicosus, Albert Torquatus, Strader, Capesius, Felix Balde, Felicia Balde, Romanus, Maria, Johannes Thomasius and Theodora appear in the spirit region of Scenes 5 and 6 as souls and in the Temple of Scenes 7 and 8 as personalities living in a far-distant past.

In regard to *The Soul's Awakening*, a remark may be added similar to that made about the preceding soul-portrayals. Neither the spiritual and soul events nor the spiritual beings are intended to be mere symbols or allegories. To anyone interpreting them as such, the real character and being of the spiritual world will remain closed.

Even in the appearance of personalities as thought-forms (Scenes 2, 3 and 10), nothing is portrayed merely symbolically; they are genuine experiences of the soul as real for the one who enters the spiritual world as are persons or events in the physical world. For such a person this Awakening presents a completely realistic soul-portrayal. Had it been a question of symbols or allegories, I should certainly have left these scenes unwritten.

In response to various questions, I considered adding a few supplementary remarks in explanation of this whole soul-portrayal. But again, as on former occasions, I suppress the attempt. I am averse to adding material of this kind to a portrayal intended to speak for itself. Such abstractions do not play any part in the conception and elaboration of the portrayal. They would only have a disturbing effect. The spiritual reality here depicted presents itself to the soul as convincingly as the objects of physical observation. It lies in the nature of such a portrayal that a sound spiritual vision relates the images of spiritual perception to beings and events quite differently than the perceptions of the physical world relate to physical beings and events. On the other hand, it must be said that the manner in which spiritual events present themselves to inner perception contains implicitly the character, disposition and composition of such a portrayal.

Rudolf Steiner
*Munich, August 1913**

---

*Translation by R & H Pusch, 1973. Revised by A.L. & M.B., 1994.

SCENE 1

The office of Hilary Gottgetreu, not very modern in style. From its appearance it can be seen that Hilary is the owner of a sawmill. The Secretary and the Manager are discussing the contents of some letters.

SECRETARY   And here's one from our friends in Georgebury.
            Now *they're* dissatisfied as well.

MANAGER   Them as well? It's deplorable!
            And always the same reasons!
            Reading between the lines, you can see
            how difficult it is for these loyal customers
            to have to take their business elsewhere.

SECRETARY   'Lacking in punctuality ...'
            'Workmanship not up to the standards of your
                competitors in the field ...'
            All these letters are full of the same complaints.
            And they're exactly the things I'm always having to
                hear on my business-trips.
            This firm was handed down to us with a solid
                reputation.
            But now, instead of growing more prestigious,
            our good name is being dragged into the dirt.
            And we're being tainted with the opinion—which is
                growing—
            that our general manager is being hoodwinked by
                visionaries and cranks,
            and that through his ever-increasing fanaticism
            he is losing the quality of conscientiousness,
            which always made the products of his firm so well
                renowned.
            As many people who once praised our work
            now criticise it.

MANAGER	For a long time it's been patently obvious
how Hilary lets himself be led astray
by people engaged in a particular kind of spiritual research.
He always had such inclinations,
but formerly he was able to keep them separate from his daily life.

(Enter Hilary.)

I think it's time I had a little talk with the chief—alone.

(Exit Secretary.)

Something is troubling me ...
Would this be a suitable moment to have a rather serious word with you?

HILARY	Well yes of course, my friend. What's troubling you?

MANAGER	Many signs are making it quite clear to me
that our production is steadily declining.
We are falling short of what we should achieve.
The voices of complaint are growing louder.
People say the quality of our products is deteriorating
and that our competitors are outdoing us.
Many deplore—quite rightly in my opinion—
the breakdown of our punctuality,
which was once the hallmark of our firm.
If this continues, even our best of friends
will no longer be satisfied with us.

HILARY	I have long been aware of everything you say.
Quite frankly, it doesn't really worry me.
However, I think I owe it to you to discuss in full the situation.
For to me, you're not just an employee of my firm,

but a loyal friend who has stood by me through thick
    and thin.
Therefore, I shall now clearly state to you
what I have often merely hinted at.

He who would create the new
must be able to endure the passing of the old
in full tranquillity.
In future, I do not intend to direct the work as has
    been done till now.
To make a profit, which benefits only a few,
by manufacturing commodities determined solely
    by the whims of the market,
and without a thought for the consequences—
this seems to me undignified.
I will not do it!
For I have seen how work can be ennobled
when it is taken hold of by people who are active in
    the spirit.
From now on, Thomasius will be made artistic
    director
of the workshops I intend to build for him nearby.
In this way, what we can produce mechanically
will receive artistic form through him.
And so we will be able to supply products for
    everyday use,
which are both practical and beautiful.
Industry and Art will work together
to bring good taste and quality to daily life.
Thus into this *corpse*—for so our work appears to me
    at present—
I shall breathe a soul,
and at last give meaning to our work.

MANAGER *(after some reflection)*
The idea of such a wonderful enterprise
goes quite against the spirit of our times.
Today, one can only hope to achieve perfection
through rigorous specialization.

In real life, the powers that connect each single part
    to the whole
do so in an entirely *impersonal* way;
quite automatically they allocate to each separate
    part
a value which your knowledge simply cannot give.
And anyway, even if this isn't a stumbling-block to
    you,
I still don't believe your aim could ever be achieved.
You've thought it all out beautifully.
But to find the people who will bring it down to
    earth—
I don't believe you can!

HILARY   My friend, you know I'm not a dreamer.
I would never have set myself such high aims,
had not a good star brought to me
someone who will make real my aspirations.
And I'm quite amazed you haven't seen
that *Strader* is the man.
One who has come to know him in his deepest
    being,
and who has a sense for highest human dignity,
should not be called a dreamer,
if he feels obliged to take upon himself
the task of creating for this man a field of work.

MANAGER *(surprised)*
You expect me to believe that *Strader* is the one?
Is he not a living example of how human thinking
    can go astray
when it loses its grasp of reality?
That his machine originated in genuine spiritual
    inspiration—
I do not doubt.
And if one day it can be realized,
then it'll certainly have the good effects
which Strader prematurely hoped it would.
But for a long time it will remain only a model,
because the forces which he needs to make it work

	have not yet been discovered.
	It saddens me that you could think
	that any good would ever come from entrusting your work to this man.
	Hasn't he just gone completely off the rails with this daring invention of his?
	No doubt his work led him into lofty heights of thought;
	these always will entice the human mind.
	But we should only attempt to scale these heights,
	when we have found the necessary strength.
HILARY	But see! You've had to praise the man
	while seeking reasons to dismiss him.
	This only affirms to me his worth.
	According to your own words, it was not *his* fault
	that his invention didn't succeed.
	Surely, therefore, this community of ours,
	where nothing from outside can hinder him,
	is the right place for him to be.
MANAGER	And even if I try to think like you and put aside all my objections,
	I still can't go along with you.
	For who will there be to appreciate what you produce
	and show sufficient understanding to make use of it?
	All your capital will be swallowed up
	before you've even begun production.
	And then where will you be!
HILARY	It's quite clear to me that my ideas
	would indeed contain a fatal flaw,
	if they weren't met by sufficient understanding
	for such an entirely new way of working.
	The work of Strader and Thomasius must be carried out in the place
	which I shall found to foster knowledge of the spirit.
	And meanwhile, what Benedictus, Capesius and Maria will be revealing there

> will inspire human beings with the need
> to imbue their lives with spiritual knowledge.

MANAGER
> All this will be very nice for your own little clique.
> You'll be living for yourselves alone, far away from
>   the real world,
> closing yourselves off from the rest of humanity.
> And though you'll be striving to conquer egoism,
> in actual fact you will be nurturing it.

HILARY
> You seem to see me as somebody
> who thoughtlessly denies the experiences life has
>   brought him.
> This is precisely what I would be doing,
> if for a single moment I were to adopt *your* idea of
>   success.
> What is of value to *me* may indeed fail outwardly.
> But even if it falls to pieces because the whole world
>   ridicules it,
> nevertheless, an example for humanity
> would have—just once—been placed upon the
>   earth.
> In spirit it will work on,
> even if it does not survive in earthly life.
> And it will have contributed to the earth a small part
>   of the power,
> which will one day bring about the marriage of
>   spiritual goals with earthly deeds.
> This is what spiritual knowledge teaches us.

MANAGER
> At first, I only wanted to approach you
> with what I felt duty-bound to discuss as an
>   employee of your firm.
> But now, your frankness has encouraged me
> to approach you also as a friend.
> Many years ago, I first felt an urge
> to acquire knowledge of the things with which you
>   concern yourself
> and to which you give your energy.
> I could only find my instruction in books—

books which attempted to disclose spiritual knowledge.
Although the worlds they directed me towards are inaccessible to me,
I was able to get some idea of how those human beings must feel
who devote themselves faithfully to such spiritual disciplines.
Through my own research, I confirmed
what many experts in this field clearly describe
about the type of person who feels at home in the spiritual world.
Above all else it struck me
that, in spite of all precautions,
when such people have to leave the high realms of their spiritual experience
and return to earth,
they're not able to distinguish between reality and illusion.
Out of the spiritual world in which they have been living,
certain apparitions arise
that cloud their perception of the physical world
and weaken the power of judgement necessary for their daily life.

HILARY Your objections only strengthen my belief,
that in you I have someone I can count on as a colleague in my future plans.
How could I ever have guessed
that you'd have made yourself familiar
with the inner disposition of the kind of people wanting to join me in my endeavours.
Just because you understand the dangers that can threaten them,
you'll be able to observe their actions
and perceive how they've also learnt the ways to protect themselves.
You'll soon understand the situation.

                And then I'll have my good advisor back with me
                    again—
                the man I simply cannot do without!

MANAGER   I just cannot put myself into any kind of work
                whose methods are not clear to me.
                The people in whom you've put your trust
                seem to me to be entangled in the very kind of
                    illusion of which I spoke.
                And those who listen to them will be led astray as
                    well,
                until their faculty to make decisions for themselves
                will be completely smothered and destroyed.
                You will always find me at your side,
                ready and willing to give you my advice,
                for as long as you intend to base your work
                upon the firm foundation of earthly reality.
                But your new way of work is not for me!

HILARY   By your refusal, you jeopardize the work
                that is trying to serve a noble spiritual aim.
                Without your good advice, I shall be lamed.
                Just think how one's sense of responsibility must
                    grow,
                when in the convergence of all these human beings
                one can recognize—as I have done—
                a sign of destiny.

MANAGER   The more you lecture me like this,
                the more I am convinced that unknown to yourself
                you have already fallen prey to error.
                You think you render service to humanity,
                when actually you serve the members of a sect,
                whose spiritual dream can only last a short while
                    longer
                because of your support.
                This place will soon be turned into a hive of activity.
                These 'chosen' human beings will no doubt see this
                    as *spiritually ordained,*
                but *we* will see it as a phantom of hot air

through which the fruits of all our years of labour are
    destroyed!

HILARY   If you'll not give me your support,
          the prospects do indeed seem bleak.

(Enter Strader from stage-left.)

          Ah, Strader, I've been expecting you ...
          Something has just come up which ...
              I think ...
          would make it best if we postponed our walk
              together,
          and had a serious conversation instead.
          My old friend here has just confided in me
          that he cannot go along with what we've planned.
          So ... let's hear from the man himself
          who *has* promised to give our work his full support.
          Much now depends upon how human beings
          can find each other; for as separate worlds
          we stand in confrontation, each alone.
          But if the gulf between us can be bridged,
          great good may be created for the world.

STRADER   Am I to believe that such a loyal colleague
          does not intend to put himself behind the promising
              work,
          which has arisen out of your far-sightedness?
          In truth, we can succeed
          only when aims seeking to serve the future
          unite in the right way with well-tested practical
              experience.

MANAGER   I not only intend to hold myself back from your
              work,
          but also I would like to prove to my dear friend
          the complete futility of his venture!

STRADER   I'm not at all surprised that you should think
that any enterprise connected to the name of
 'Strader'
is already doomed to fail.
I've had to witness the collapse of an even greater
 project,
because the forces that were needed to make it work
are still hidden in our time—
though in its basic conception it was quite sound.
The well-known fact that I owe my invention to
 spiritual insight,
and that although in theory it was correct
it could not be realized,
undermines people's belief in my faculty of
 judgement
and kills their faith in the spirit as a source of true
 creativity in the world.

It will be difficult to convince you that my past
 experiences
give me the strength to avoid falling into error a
 second time.
I *had* to go astray then,
in order to learn how this time to keep clear
of the many pitfalls lying in wait along the path to
 truth.

It's quite understandable that you have doubts.
One who thinks as you do will find it especially hard
 to believe
that anything at all could ever come from our way of
 working.

People speak highly of the sensitive and discerning
 way you participate in cultural life,
supporting it with your time and energy.
But it's also clear you like to see your working life
 kept strictly separate
from the spiritual life you cultivate outside your
 working hours.

	However, to combine spiritual activity with work in the material world— *this* is the goal of that spiritual stream which gives me my direction in life.

MANAGER	So long as spiritual activity remains within the
	    spiritual sphere alone,
	human beings will be ennobled and find meaning in
	    their lives.
	But when it also tries to have an influence on
	    material existence,
	it trespasses upon a realm
	where all sense for truth is threatened by illusion.
	I have gained this insight through my own efforts in
	    understanding spiritual matters.
	And it is *this* that has formed my attitude today—
	not my natural inclinations, as you've wrongly
	    assumed
	from what you've heard of me.

STRADER	So then it is a *spiritual* error
	which makes you oppose my views with such
	    hostility.
	I fear our difficulties will grow more and more.
	It's relatively easy for the spiritual researcher
	to work in partnership with other human beings,
	who have already learnt the truths of existence
	through nature and through life.
	But when *both* partners claim their thoughts are
	    spiritually inspired,
	yet actually come into conflict when they attempt to
	    unite—
	then harmony can seldom be achieved.
	
	(Pause.)
	
	And yet ... what must be *will* be.
	
	Another study of my plans
	will ... perhaps ... make you change the opinion

which, from your first considerations, you have formed.

(Curtain, while each stands fixed in thought.)

SCENE 2

A mountain landscape. In the background, Hilary's house in the vicinity of the sawmill. On the left—a waterfall. Johannes and, unknown to him, Capesius.

JOHANNES Rock walls, rising steeply from the earth—
their towering presence here ... so full of silence ...
surrounds me with a sense of deepest mystery.
No painful questions, deadening and dull,
arise here for the soul that has no wish to *know*,
but only to drink in all that Nature livingly reveals.
Around these rocks ... a flickering play of light—
their bare, flat surfaces ... their silent strength.
And here, the forest ... green shades darkening into blue.
This is the world in which Johannes' soul
would stay awhile and weave in vivid dream
the pictures of a magic time-to-come.

Johannes' soul must feel within itself
the depths and widths of this majestic world.
Creative powers will then release in him
capacities to reveal to human hearts
the magic of the world, transformed through art.

But all this would be quite beyond Johannes
without Maria, who with her gentle warmth,
awakens through her love his inner strength.
I thank the powers of destiny for bringing me so close to her.
And yet, how short the time that she has been with me!
How deep the bond which in these weeks has formed!
I feel her spiritually alive within me,
even when she herself is far away.

And when I turn my inner eye to distant goals of life,
she thinks within my thinking.

(Maria appears as a thought-form of Johannes.)

Maria? Is this she? But look at her!
She should not appear like this to me:
her face so stern, her bearing so austere.
It turns my blood to ice.
Johannes will not see it.
He cannot bear to have her near him in this form.
It cannot be the same Maria
who, by careful guidance of the powers of destiny,
was led into my life.

(Maria vanishes from Johannes' vision.)

Where is Maria—the one who loved Johannes as he used to be,
before she transformed his soul and led it into frosty heights of spirit?

But now, Johannes too, the one who loved Maria—
where is *he*? He was here just now,
restoring me to myself so wonderfully!
But now I have lost sight of him completely.
The past has cruelly robbed me of him—
this cannot be!

(Maria again becomes visible to Johannes.)

MARIA
Maria, in the form you wish to see her,
does not exist in worlds where truth prevails.
The spirit of Johannes,
led on by the illusions in his soul,
is entering into regions of untruth.
Free yourself from the power of your wishes!
They are seducing you.
I feel the tempest of your soul in me.
It robs me of the peace I need.

SCENE 2

              It's not Johannes who sends this storm into my soul.
              It is another being.
              Long ago Johannes conquered it within himself.
              But now in phantom-form it roams through widths
                  of spirit-space.
              Recognize it!
              It will be scattered into nothingness.

JOHANNES   So *this* is the true Maria!
              She speaks of Johannes as he now can really see
                  himself to be.
              For a long time he was able to raise himself into a
                  higher state of being,
              than that which this deceptive play of dreams paints
                  for me now.
              I have allowed myself to be lulled
              into a drowsy state of comfortable inertia.

              But this state does not yet have complete control of
                  me.
              I can still free myself from it.
              I *will*!
              It often draws me to itself;
              with all its power it desires to possess me.
              But still I feel impelled to separate myself from it.
              For many years, it filled the depths of my
                  unconscious soul.
              And yet—I do not want to know it now!

              You alien being inhabiting Johannes' soul,
              let go of me!
              Give me back myself as I once was
              before you began to work in me.
              I wish to see Johannes
              without your interfering presence.

              (Benedictus, also as a thought-form of Johannes,
              appears beside Maria.)

BENEDICTUS   Johannes, listen to the voice of warning in your soul!
             The One who rises in you now as primal power of
                 your being
             and fills you with his spiritual strength—
             he must abide within you faithfully,
             demanding from you that in your acts of will
             you humanize the power that streams from him.
             Hidden within you he must work,
             that one day you become the being now given to you
             as image of your distant goal.
             You must guard within yourself the personal
                 concerns which weigh you down
             and bear them silently through life.
             You'll gain yourself when you courageously
                 surrender to this being
             and let him fill you more and more.

MARIA   My sacred vow is radiating strength to you,
             that you hold fast to what you have achieved.
             You find me in the frozen fields of ice,
             where spirits must themselves create the light
             when darkness lames the powers of life.
             Now seek me in the deepest ground of worlds,
             where souls win back their feeling for the gods
             by wresting from the void—new being.
             But do not seek me in the realm of shades,
             where tattered remnants of the soul, through fraud,
             make fleeting parody of being.
             And dreams of illusion envelop the one,
             who, sunk in self-indulgent sleep,
             has chosen to forget himself,
             because true spirit-mindfulness seems too much
                 trouble!

             (Benedictus and Maria disappear.)

JOHANNES   She speaks of illusion ...
             And yet ... how beautiful is this illusion!
             It is alive. Johannes feels himself in it.
             He feels Maria close to him as well.

> Johannes does not want to know
> how in the dark depths of the soul
> enigmas are illumined through the spirit's light.
> He will create! As artist he will work!
> So let all yearning to perceive the higher worlds in consciousness
> be buried in him.
>
> *(He sinks into himself. Capesius stands up, coming back to himself from deep contemplation.)*

CAPESIUS
> Did I not clearly experience within myself just now,
> how in a dream Johannes wove around himself
> the pictures of his longing?
> Thoughts flashed up in me which were not mine;
> they belonged to him;
> *his* inner being was living here within me.
> He looked younger, seeing himself in the mirror of illusion,
> as he belittled the achievements of his spiritual life.
>
> What can this mean?
> Why at this moment am I witness to these things?
> It is a rare event when pupils of the spirit
> behold within themselves another's being!
>
> I've often heard from Benedictus
> that this may happen—for a short time—
> only when a pupil has been chosen by the grace of destiny
> to be raised one step higher on his spiritual path.
> Dare I now apply this to myself?
> Something so unusual ... indeed,
> something that could never be an everyday event,
> for how dreadful it would be if all the time
> the seer was forced to eavesdrop into other people's inner lives!
> Did I see truly?
> Or was it an illusion,

                which forced on me this dream about another
                    person's soul?
                Only from Johannes can I know for sure.

                (Capesius approaches Johannes who now becomes aware of him.)

JOHANNES   Capesius ... I thought that you were far away from here ...

CAPESIUS   But I felt close to you!

JOHANNES   Close to me? Just now, you mean?

CAPESIUS   Why should this disturb you?

JOHANNES   Disturb me? Not at all. It's only ...

                (Enter Maria.)

JOHANNES *(to himself)*
                His gaze ... He sees right into the depths of my soul!

CAPESIUS *(to himself)*
                He *was* disturbed—I did see truly ...

                Maria, you appear at the right time.
                Perhaps you can solve the problem that is weighing on me.

MARIA   I expected to see Johannes here, not you.
                I thought I'd find the problem weighing on *him*.
                You, however, I believed to be happily devoted to the project
                which Hilary is making possible for us.

CAPESIUS   This project—what has it to do with me?
                It's just a source of irritation to me now.

SCENE 2

MARIA A source of irritation? Surely, you must be delighted
that your hopes at last can be fulfilled!

CAPESIUS What has happened to me just now, in this
significant moment in my life,
changes everything completely!
Any kind of preoccupation with earthly affairs
would impair my newly awakened clairvoyant
faculties.

MARIA Whoever treads the spiritual path
will be exposed to various beckonings of destiny.
These he may well choose to follow as directions of
his inner life.
But if they interfere with his earthly duties,
they cannot have been properly interpreted.

*(Capesius sits and falls briefly into a state of
contemplation. Lucifer appears to Maria.)*

LUCIFER Your efforts are in vain!
Within his heart powers are already stirring
that give me entrance.
Maria, with your strength of spirit-vision,
look into the depths of this man's soul.
See how he ascends on wings of spirit,
freeing himself from the earthly task
that you so warmly embrace with all your love.

*(Lucifer remains in the landscape. As Maria turns
decisively to Capesius to rouse him from his
contemplation, he comes to himself of his own accord.)*

MARIA If Johannes were to feel *his* duties as a disturbance to
his spiritual path,
it would not be right, but at least it would be
understandable.
For he must work outwardly.
But *your* task is to expound to others knowledge of
the spirit,

| | and therefore there will be no need for you
to leave the sphere in which you are at home. |

CAPESIUS   Spiritual power is far more readily diffused
in words than in outer work.
For words compel us to conceptualize what we see,
and concepts are opposed to powers of seership.
The spiritual experience I had was only possible
because the soul that was revealed to me
belonged to one whom—though I knew him well—
I'd never fully understood.
If this experience is true,
then nothing in the world will bind me to your work.
For then I'll have to feel that mighty powers of
    destiny
are pointing to quite other aims than those which
    Hilary has in mind for me.

Johannes, be honest with me.
Just now, when you were absorbed in inner
    contemplation,
did you not feel that wishes from your past
lived in you once more as if they were your present
    self?

JOHANNES   Is it really possible that my spiritual confusion
could become the inner experience of someone else?
And does an error grow so strong when it is seen
that it can find its way into the stream of world
    events?

(Johannes sinks again into contemplation. Maria turns her gaze to Lucifer and hears him speak.)

LUCIFER   Here too I find an entry to the soul!
I will not waste this opportunity.
If there arises in *this* soul as well
desires for the spirit,
then must the work of love,
which from Hilary now threatens me,

SCENE 2

be ruined utterly!
Through Johannes I can destroy Maria's power.
Then all that she achieves will fall to me!

(Exit Lucifer. Capesius stands up and speaks with ever-greater confidence.)

CAPESIUS   All doubt has vanished. Yes ... I did see truly.
It really was the inner experience of Johannes that I saw.
And it is now perfectly clear:
his inner world revealed itself to me,
because I never sought to approach him intellectually.
The path to the spirit demands strict solitude.
It is only people who interact by means of concepts who can work together.
He who wishes to reach the wide horizons of the worlds of light,
must keep himself remote from other human beings.

I see in Father Felix my example.
He seeks in proud seclusion for the spirit's light
on paths which seem quite strange to other human beings.
His striving has brought him rich rewards,
just because he has always been careful to avoid
having to grasp things intellectually.
From now on, I will follow him.
Capesius no longer feels drawn into your work,
which would only drag his clairvoyance down
with the weight of earth.

(Exit Capesius.)

MARIA   This is what happens to human beings
when their better self sinks into spirit-sleep
and they are fed by powers of desire—
until they awaken to their true spirit-nature
and once more shine with light.

It is the sleep which all human beings sleep
before their spirit's eye is opened.
They have no inkling of their waking-sleep;
they seem awake—because they always sleep.
And when the seer takes leave of his true being
and wakes as others do,
this wakening—he knows—is spirit-sleep.

Capesius will now withdraw from us.
It's no passing whim that drives him from our goals;
it's something deeply-seated in his nature.
And that he turns away from us is not his doing.
One sees in it clear signs of destiny.
And so, we others who remain
must devote ourselves even more strongly to the work.

JOHANNES
Maria, do not demand from Johannes
that he arm himself just now for further tasks.
His soul still *needs* the sleep Capesius sleeps,
in order that its germinating powers
be nurtured to maturity.
I know that one day I will dare to do the spirit's work,
but do not ask me to be active now ... not now!
Just think—I drove away Capesius.
If I was ready for this work—he would be too.

MARIA
You drove away Capesius? You're dreaming!

JOHANNES
Yes ... but my dream was *conscious*;
I was *awake* while dreaming.
What appeared to cosmic powers as illusion
symbolized to me the stage I've reached in my development.
I am quite sure: I myself was my wishing,
and it was only my thinking that was another self.
This is how Johannes appeared to me—
as he used to be, before the spirit took hold of him
and filled him with a second higher self.

He is not dead.
The living power of wish within Johannes
has made him the companion of my soul.
I have stunned him, but I have not yet conquered him.
And when my higher self must sink in sleep,
he rises again and claims his right to exist!
This higher self in me—it cannot always be awake.
And it was sleeping at that moment when Capesius could experience
how I was torn out of myself by that other being.
My dreaming became for Capesius a sign of destiny.
And so he was driven away from us
by a power that worked in *me*, not him—
a power that prohibits us
from bringing spiritual activity into earthly work.

MARIA
Primal powers approach us. Summon them!
Direct your gaze to depths of world-foundations.
Wait until the powers that work there
feel what stirs within your deepest being
in kinship to themselves.
They conjure up before your inner eye
the power that makes you one with them.
Silence the clamour of your mind.
With spiritual beings you'll then be able to commune.
Listen to what they say.
Their words will bear you to the spheres of light
and bind you to reality in spirit.
What from bygone times now dawns in you
will stand before you in full clarity of light.
It will compel you then no longer,
for what is known to you, you can consciously direct.
Compare it with elemental beings,
with shadows and demons, with spectres of all kinds.
And so experience it for what it really is.
But grasp your deepest being in spirit-realms,

where primal power to primal power is bound,
where forces work to quicken growth of worlds,
where universal aims are given their direction.
Such cosmic vision will give you strength
amidst the surging ocean of the spirit
to unite your inmost being with the Being of the
    world.

It was the Spirit's will that I reveal all this to you.
Now listen to what you've known for long,
but never welded truly to your deepest being.

JOHANNES *(with great effort)*
    All right ... In spite of myself, I will listen!

(From both sides of the stage enter elemental beings. From stage-right—small, steel-grey, gnomelike beings. They are nearly all head, which droops forward, and they have long, mobile limbs, well adapted for gesturing but clumsy for walking. From stage-left—slim, nearly headless, sylphlike forms, their feet and hands something between fins and wings. Some of them are yellow-red with sharply-outlined figures; the others are blue-green and less defined. The words spoken by all these beings are accompanied by expressive gestures, which develop into dance.)

CHORUS OF GNOMES
    We harden, we strengthen
    the glittering, dusty matter.
    We loosen, we crumble
    the stiff and crusty strata.
    We quickly sand the hard-stuff,
    and slowly fasten loose-stuff,
    with bodies made of spirit
    and woven out of thinking-matter—
    already quick and clever,
    when sleepy human beings
    at earth's beginning still were dreaming.

SCENE 2

CHORUS OF SYLPHS
    We weave, we unravel
    the airy water-surges.
    We sunder, we scatter
    the living sun-force in the seed.
    With care we densify light-power,
    and wisely lessen strength of ripening,
    with bodies, soul-enwoven
    and flowing out from radiant feeling,
    which ever-living glimmers,
    that human beings living
    find joy in earth-becoming's meaning.

CHORUS OF GNOMES
    We laugh and we chuckle,
    we mock and we snigger,
    when human beings stumbling,
    with human senses fumbling,
    perceive what we've created
    and think their brains can comprehend it.
    When really spirits working
    have conjured it before their stupid staring.

CHORUS OF SYLPHS
    We nurture, we cherish,
    we ripen, we quicken,
    when children into life first entering,
    and aged ones in error weaving,
    are nourished by our working,
    in childlike wonder or in old-age dreaming,
    and dimly joy within the stream of time
    what we through all eternity are tending.

(These elemental beings form two clusters and remain visible in the background. From stage-right the three soul-forces appear—Philia, Astrid and Luna—with the Other Philia.)

PHILIA
    They radiate brightness
    as loving light-bringers

in blissful maturing.
They gently are warming
and forcefully heating,
where strength of becoming
is striving for being;
that being, when attained,
bring joy to the souls,
who gladly surrender
to streaming of light.

ASTRID
In life they are weaving
as helpers creative
in swelling of being.
The earth they break open,
the air they so thicken,
that changes may follow
in striving-creating;
that striving-creating
give joy to the spirits,
who feel themselves weaving,
creative in life.

LUNA
With care they are moulding
the malleable matter
as active creators.
They sharpen the edges,
they flatten each surface,
as wisely they labour
in looming of forms;
that looming of forms
take hold of the will,
which labours in wisdom
with fire to create.

OTHER PHILIA
They pluck from the blossoms
in carefree abandon
for magical working.
The truth they are dreaming,
illusion they're guarding,

that seeds which have slumbered
are wakened to life;
and wakening-dreaming
to souls is revealing
the enchanted weaving
of their own inmost being.

(Exit stage-left the four soul-forces, together with the elemental beings. Johannes awakens from deep contemplation.)

JOHANNES
'And wakening-dreaming
to souls is revealing
the enchanted weaving
of their own inmost being.'

These words still clearly resound within me,
while all that I saw before
has retreated from me in confusion.

But what is it that I feel stirring in me,
when I hear these words again?
'... the enchanted weaving
of their own inmost being.'

(He falls again into meditation. Before him, as his own thought-form, there appears the Spirit of Johannes' Youth with Lucifer at its left side and the soul of Theodora at its right side.)

SPIRIT OF JOHANNES' YOUTH
I feed upon the substance of your wishes;
I breathe into my being your youthful dreams.
I can exist only when you do not desire
to enter worlds where I can't follow you.
If you forget that I am part of you,
I'll have to suffer pain
and serve the evil ends of cruel, unfeeling shadows.
Sustainer of my life—do not abandon me!

LUCIFER	Abandon you? This he will never do!
For I can see within his being's depths
desires for light that never will submit unto Maria's guidance.
When these desires, with all their shining splendour,
fully illumine his creative soul,
then he'll no longer wish to waste their fruits
in realms where love would rule bereft of beauty.
Imagine how he'll feel towards that Self,
who, for the sake of knowledge,
would throw his finest forces to the shades.
When wisdom's light will one day shine within his wishes,
they'll be revealed to him in all their glory.
So long as they remain submerged in darkness,
he'll fail to see the value they possess for him.
Until that time when the light of wisdom can penetrate to his desires,
I will be your true protector.
I will achieve this through the light that I can find in depths of human souls.

Johannes still lacks mercy for your sufferings.
For when he is engaged in lofty, light-filled striving,
he always lets you sink into the shades.
He fails to see that you—his poor, forgotten child—
must lead a spell-bound, solitary life of pain.
But from now on, you shall have *me* beside you
in those hard times when, through his guilt,
you're driven as a shadow to the frozen wastelands of neglect.
And when he flies away to spirit-realms,
then, with the right that Lucifer has preserved from laws of ancient worlds,

(with the word 'Lucifer', the Spirit of Johannes' Youth trembles violently)

I will take hold of all he leaves unguarded in his depths. |

          This treasure I'll then bring to you,
          that it may ease the burden of your solitude
          inflicted on you by the realm of shades.
          However, you will only be released from your
              enchantment,
          when he once more unites himself to you.
          He can delay this—but he cannot prevent it.
          For Lucifer will have his ancient rights!

THEODORA You spirit-child, who in the dark realm of the shades
          lives out Johannes' youth:
          from realms of light and warmth,
          there lovingly inclines to you that soul who is
              Johannes' protector.
          From your enchantment she will set you free.
          If you will take into yourself what streams in feeling
              from her,
          you'll gain a life of blessedness.
          I shall unite you with the beings of the elements,
          who work unconsciously in the surrounding world,
          forever drawing back from human wakefulness.
          With spirits of the earth, you will create in form;
          you'll ray out forces with the souls of fire;
          but only if you sacrifice your conscious life
          unto the Will which radiates its light-filled strength
          in depths where human understanding cannot
              reach.
          In doing this, you will protect from Lucifer
          that knowledge which is only partly yours.
          You will be able then to serve Johannes worthily.
          Out of his depths of soul, I'll bring to you
          what causes him to need you still
          and gives to him refreshing spirit-sleep.

LUCIFER   But *beauty* she can never offer you,
          for in defiance I will snatch it from her!

THEODORA I will ensure that beauty spring from pure and light-
              filled feelings,
          and that it ripen in the work of sacrifice.

LUCIFER   But your free will, she'll rob from you
          and deliver you to powers who rule in darkness!

THEODORA I will awaken the power to see true,
          that vision be set free—even from Lucifer!

          (Lucifer, Theodora and the Spirit of Johannes' Youth disappear. Johannes, awakening from meditation, sees the Other Philia approaching him.)

OTHER PHILIA
          'And wakening-dreaming
          to souls is revealing
          the enchanted weaving
          of their own inmost being.'

JOHANNES Mysterious spirit—through your words
          I stepped into this world.
          Yet only one of all its wonders
          seems important to me now.
          That shadow, who appeared to me with Lucifer and Theodora—
          does it exist in the spiritual world as a real, living being?

OTHER PHILIA
          It lives—through you it has been awakened to existence.
          Just as the things that light lets fall upon the surface of a mirror
          are shown there merely as reflected images,
          so must the things that you behold in spiritual worlds,
          before you have attained the right to see them face to face,
          be livingly reflected to you in a world of half-unconscious shadow-beings.

JOHANNES It's just an image then? ... created by myself?

OTHER PHILIA
>Yet one that *lives*, and will live on
>so long as you will not let go
>of that within you which you've long out-grown.
>Although you certainly can stun it,
>you've not been able yet to conquer it.
>Johannes, your awakening will remain illusion,
>until that time when you yourself set free
>the Shadow, who through your guilt
>is forced to lead a spell-bound life.

JOHANNES Now thanks be to this mysterious spirit.
It brings me good advice,
and I will follow it!

(Slow curtain, while the Other Philia and Johannes remain motionless.)

SCENE 3

The same landscape as in the preceding scene. Magnus Bellicosus, Romanus, Torquatus and Hilary enter from stage-left, deep in conversation.

BELLICOSUS And if his colleague remains so fixed in his ideas,
how is the work ever going to succeed,
which out of his good heart Hilary is trying to do for the world?

ROMANUS The Manager's objections are not only relevant
to those who base their opinions upon the facts of outer life.
Surely, they are quite in harmony
with the opinions formed from occult facts as well.

BELLICOSUS But they have no place within that circle of friends
who have *our* aims at heart.
We were succeeded in our mystic work by the pupils of Benedictus;
and now Hilary wants to create for them the work
through which their ideals may become reality.
Wise powers of destiny have united them to us within the Temple;
and Hilary is merely carrying out the orders,
which were given to us there as our duty to the spirit.

ROMANUS But are you quite sure that you've interpreted these orders correctly?
Wouldn't it be more convincing to suggest
that Benedictus himself—along with his pupils—
should remain within the inner Temple,
and not yet tread the difficult path to which Hilary wants to lead them?
Even for him, spiritual vision may all too easily slip
into a sleepy, atavistic state.

BELLICOSUS   I would never have expected to hear a view like that from you!
I could accept it coming from someone like the Manager,
who can only get his knowledge—which is of very dubious value—
out of books.
But *you* are obliged to be able to read the signs
that appear to one who treads the spiritual path.
The way in which the pupils of Benedictus were led to us
is a clear indication.
They are united to us in order that we follow
what is revealed to them through their clairvoyance.

TORQUATUS   However, there is another sign that seems to indicate
that the project given to us in the Temple
has *not* received the full blessing of the spiritual world:
Capesius has separated off from Benedictus and his circle.
The fact that he cannot yet maintain
the inner wakefulness that Benedictus expects of him
casts a shadow on the *teacher's* competence as well.

BELLICOSUS   Certainly, I'm still a long way off from having any gift of real seership;
yet I do often feel that particular events release in me a kind of premonition.
And the first time I saw Capesius with us in the Temple,
a thought impressed itself upon me:
Destiny places this man in our midst
and at the same time keeps him far away from us.

ROMANUS   I can well understand your premonition.
But in that same moment, *I* somehow sensed
that of all our new colleagues

none was as closely connected to me through the
    will of destiny as Strader.
I treat such an intuition merely as a sign
pointing out to me the direction
in which by means of rational thinking I can go
    further.
And when it comes to action,
I first obliterate the intuition that initially sparked
    my thinking.
For to me, this is what the strictest occult rules
    demand.
I certainly feel myself to be closely united in spirit
    with the pupils of Benedictus.
However, it is only at *Strader's* side
that I would venture to find a way out of the inner
    Temple
back into daily life.

(Ahriman appears in the background and passes from stage-left to stage-right without being seen.)

TORQUATUS   But Hilary's Manager doesn't see in Strader
a man of confidence able to serve outer life
    effectively.
And when I listen to *my* inner voice,
it becomes apparent to me
that Strader completely lacks the correct soul-mood
    of the mystic.
Certainly, what outer life can teach him
and what his intellect can grasp of the life in spirit
arouse in him the strongest urge for research.
But he is still far away from genuine spiritual
    experience.
What is the spiritual life of such a man
but a dark and nebulous web of dreams!

ROMANUS   And yet, he has not gone far enough along the path
    his friends are treading
to become bound up with certain adversaries of the
    soul,

SCENE 3

which, if allowed to enter into sense-existence,
can be a source of great danger to pupils of the spirit.

BELLICOSUS If you believe Strader to be free of such adversaries,
then nothing is stopping you from working for him,
in order that Hilary's project can succeed.
When the Manager hears that you admire the man
whom he has such a low opinion of,
then surely his confidence in his own judgement will
    be shaken.
You're the only one who can win him over to our
    cause.
For he knows that you with your shrewd foresight
have always been successful in outer life
in everything you've ever done.

ROMANUS Hilary, my dear friend,
if you were prepared to take on Strader by himself,
keeping the rest of Benedictus' pupils at a safe
    distance from your work,
then you can be sure you'd not be left alone.
For in addition to the help that Bellicosus is now
    asking of me,
I'd be prepared to put all my assets at your disposal
to serve the excellent plan of Dr Strader!

HILARY How could you imagine that at this crucial moment
Strader would be prepared to part from the other
    pupils of Benedictus
and pursue only his *own* aims?
These friends of his are as close to him as his own
    self.

ROMANUS On a *human* level, they may well be close to him.
But it can only be that part of his soul clouded by a
    deep spiritual sleep
which could ever believe itself united to them
    spiritually as well.
And I would think that very soon we'll see
how this sleeping part of him awakens.

(They exit stage-right. From the other side enter Capesius, Strader, Felix and Felicia.)

CAPESIUS
To seek the spirit *inwardly*—
at present, this is all that I can do.
If I were to burden myself with outer work,
to make manifest the spirit in the senses' world,
I'd have to fool myself that I could grasp the
    meaning of existence
in realms that are as yet beyond my reach.

I can behold only so much of the world's reality
as has already become part of my own being.
How, then, should my work be of benefit to others,
if it were no more than a form of self-indulgence?

STRADER
If I understand you rightly, you are saying
that all creative work bears the stamp only of the
    personal being of its creator,
and that consequently, if you were to work,
you'd be giving to the world nothing more than your
    subjective self?

CAPESIUS
Indeed, until I can truly encounter a being other
    than myself,
that is how it is.
Just how little I'm now able to enter into the inner
    world of another
I painfully had to realize,
when for a moment I awakened and saw clearly.

FELIX BALDE
I've never heard you speak like this before.
And yet ... never have I understood you so well!
For now, nothing other than *yourself* is speaking.
In your words I hear the mystic mood,
which I have patiently pursued for many years.
This mood alone can apprehend the light—
the light in which, with clearest vision,
the human spirit can feel itself to be at one
with the spirit of the world.

SCENE 3

CAPESIUS Because I felt how close to you I've come,
I have escaped to you from all that turmoil and commotion
which would be sheer anathema to my inner life.

STRADER In the past I could understand you when you spoke like this.
And what you said I took for words of wisdom.
But not a word of what you're saying is making sense to me right now.
Capesius and Father Felix ... both of you
conceal dark meaning in transparent words.

Something lies behind your words ... They are but a cloak for powers ... powers within the soul ... which are thrusting me away from you to worlds remote from your way of thinking ... worlds in which I have no wish to be ... because ... in my deepest heart ... I love *your* worlds!

I can easily bear the opposition,
which from the outer world is now threatening my work.
Yes, even if it were to shatter all my hopes,
I could endure it.
But your worlds ... I cannot do without!

FELIX BALDE The spiritual world will remain forever closed
to one who tries to enter it through *seeking*.
It gave me great joy to hear you speak some time ago of your invention;
for it came to you through an act of true enlightenment
and not through any intellectual striving.
At that time you were close to the true mystic mood.
To strive for nothing ...
to rest in complete peacefulness of soul ...
one's inner being in a state of pure expectation—
this is the mystic mood.

When it arises, then one's inner self is led into the
   light.
But outer work is incompatible with such a mood.
And if you wish to work in the outer world
and try to do this out of *mysticism*,
then with mystical delusions you'll bring destructive
   chaos into life.

STRADER   I need you—but I cannot find you.
The living connection between us—you do not
   seem to value it.
How can human beings ever find each other
in work that is trying to serve the world,
if mystics won't abandon their own separate inner
   worlds?

FELIX BALDE   Something as delicate as inner vision
cannot be carried into the outer world in which you
   work
without it being immediately obliterated by that
   world's restless stimulation.
In piety, in reverence for the all-pervading presence
   of the spirit,
allowing inner vision to rest within the heart—
this is the way the mystic should approach the world
   of action.

CAPESIUS   And if he were to enter it some other way,
then it would not reveal to him the living, light-filled
   being of wisdom,
but only what works in it as error.
I was able to see into the soul of another human
   being.
I know my inner eye was not deceiving me.
But what I saw was only the *error* of that soul.
This was because my vision had been tainted
by my desire for activity in the world.

STRADER   Thus speaks Capesius, who treads the path
far in advance of me.

And yet, for *me*, spiritual vision only arises
when I devote myself to thoughts of what can be
    achieved through deeds.
And then I find myself alive with hope
that I may build up places where the spirit can
    enkindle light—
light which warmly streams through worlds of spirit
and seeks through human activity in the senses'
    world
a new home on the earth.
You wisdom-filled expanses of the spirit—
am I the son of error, not your son?

(Strader turns away from the others. In a vision, first Benedictus, then Ahriman and later Maria appear as Strader's thought-forms, though in genuine spiritual communion.)

BENEDICTUS In wisdom-filled expanses of the spirit
you seek relief from the anguish of your questioning,
in which the deepest mystery of your inner life
weighs heavily upon your earthly thinking.
Now listen—you shall hear what from the depths of
    soul
the wide expanses of the spirit are seeking to reveal
    to you through me
as answer to your prayer.
But learn to understand what you believe you know,
what you are often bold enough to put in words,
but what, within your inmost soul,
you do no more than dream.
Let flow into this dream

(Ahriman appears)

the life that from the spirit I must offer you.
But what through thinking you can gather from the
    senses' realm,
transform into the substance of a dream.
Both Father Felix and Capesius

are banishing you from the spiritual light which they
    behold.
They open an abyss between themselves and you.
Do not regret this—
look into your own abyss.

AHRIMAN   Yes, dare to look!
You will perceive what in the world's evolving
seems to you most worthy of the human spirit.
It would indeed be good for you, if others showed
    you this
in dull and drowsy sleep of soul.
But Benedictus shows it to you while you wake,
and so you kill the answer with your seeing.
Yes. Dare to look!

STRADER   I will look!

What is this? Forms ... confused ... They change
    ... They tear ... One tears at the other ... A
    battle! ... Spectres wildly rush at one another
    ... Everywhere destruction ... darkness! ...
    Out of the darkness, other shadows ... Around
    them an etheric glow ... weaving ... red ...

Now one form clearly separates from the mass ... It
    approaches me ... sent from the abyss.

(Maria appears out of the abyss.)

MARIA   What you see are demons;
build up your strength—they will be changed.
For they are not as they appear to you.
If you can hold them fast
until their spectral nature begins to shine for you,
then you will see their true significance within the
    world's evolving.
Your vision fades before they can shine forth in their
    full power.
With your own light, illumine them.

Where is your light?
You are radiating darkness.
Know the darkness that surrounds you.
Into the light you work chaotic darkness.
You feel the darkness when you are creating it.
And yet you never feel that it is *you* who are creating it.
Although you wish to forget your urge to create,
unknown to you it is at work within your being.
You are too cowardly to radiate your light.
You'd rather keep it to yourself alone.
It is only *yourself* you wish to experience in it.
You seek yourself—and seek in deep oblivion.
Dreaming, you sink into yourself.

AHRIMAN
Yes, listen to her.
She can solve your riddles for you,
but her solution will be one you *cannot* solve!
She gives you wisdom—that you may tread the path to folly!
It might indeed be good for you some other time,
when you were in the light of spirit-day.
But now she speaks to you within your dreams,
and so she kills the solution with her good advice!
Yes. Listen to her!

STRADER
What is the intention of your words, Maria?
Do they originate in light?
In *my* light?
Or is it from my darkness that they come?
Benedictus, tell me:
Who rose up from the abyss to give me counsel?

BENEDICTUS
She came to your abyss in search of you.
In such a way do spirits seek out human beings,
in order to protect them from those beings
who fashion spectres before their eyes of soul.
These spectres shroud in dark confusion
the work of cosmic powers,
that human beings can only know themselves

                    enmeshed within the net of separate self.
                    Gaze deeper into your abyss!

STRADER   What do I see now, there in the depths of my abyss?

BENEDICTUS   Behold the shadow-beings:
                    to the right, the bluish-red ones, enticing Felix.
                    And see the others, there towards the left—
                    red, gently brightening into yellow—
                    they are advancing on Capesius.
                    Both Felix and Capesius feel the power of these
                        shadow-beings;
                    and each, out of his loneliness, forges the light
                    from which deceiving shadows must retreat.

AHRIMAN   He would be doing better if he showed you your *own*
                        shadows.
                    But this he cannot do.
                    Certainly, he is not lacking in good will.
                    He only fails to know where he should look for them.
                    They stand behind you, perilously close.
                    But you yourself are hiding them from him!

STRADER   So now at my abyss I'm forced to hear
                    what seemed ridiculous to me when spoken by the
                        Manager.

MARIA   Father Felix tempers for himself
                    the weapons by which he'll ward off threatening
                        dangers.
                    But one who treads the path which *you* must tread
                    has need of other weapons.
                    And the sword Capesius is forging for himself—
                    the sword with which he'll fight against the
                        adversaries of his soul—
                    would not be right for *you*.
                    In *your* hands it would change into a shadow-sword
                    at the first blow of your spiritual battle—
                    that battle preordained by powers of destiny,
                    for those whose task it is

to transform the ripening spirit into earthly deeds.
You cannot use *their* weapons.
But you must learn to know them,
that you may rightly forge your own
out of the substance of your soul.

(The forms of Benedictus, Ahriman and Maria disappear. Strader recovers from his spiritual vision and looks around for the others. He sits down on a rock.)

FELIX BALDE My dear Strader. It seemed to me just now
that you were transported far away from us in spirit...
Was this not the case?

(He pauses. When Strader does not reply, he continues.)

I didn't mean to be unkind
and coldly drive you away from us onto other paths of life.
I merely wanted to prevent you falling further into error.
What is perceived in spirit
should only be experienced in a purely *spiritual* way.
Take, for example, the beings of Felicia's fairy-tales.
They live for her as pure soul-beings
and therefore wish to be perceived only by eyes of soul.
How foolish it would be if she wanted them
to go dancing about in some puppet-theatre!
All their magic would be completely lost.

FELICIA BALDE
I've held my tongue for long enough!
But when you choose to bless even my fairy-folk
with your 'mystic mood',
then I must speak!
I'm sure they're very grateful to you
for first sucking all their power out of them,

and then puffing them back to life again with
    mystical hot air.
All due respect to mysticism,
but please—keep it away from my land of fairy-tales!

CAPESIUS   Felicia, was it not your fairy-tales
that first directed me towards the spirit?
The air and water beings
which you so often called up before my thirsting
    soul—
they were the first messengers of that world
which I now seek through mysticism.

FELICIA BALDE

    That may be so;
    but ever since you've brought your new mystical
        ways into our house
    you seldom ask about my magic beings.
    The ones who look severe and dignified
    may now and then be graced with your approval.
    But those who, merrily and full of fun,
    delight in dancing or in making mischief,
    seem somehow to upset your mystic mood.

CAPESIUS   No doubt, Felicia, the deeper meaning of those
        wonderful beings,
who reveal their wisdom in a playful fashion,
will also one day be revealed to me.
But at the moment, my strength is not quite up to
    seeing it ...

FELIX BALDE   Felicia, you know how much I love your fairy-folk.
But to imagine them embodied in the form of
    puppets—
this is to me quite distasteful.

FELICIA BALDE

    I haven't tried to discuss this with you yet—
    you are above such things!
    But I was happy when I first heard of Strader's plan,

and that Johannes, too, was attempting to reveal the
    spirit in material form.
I imagined all my fairy-princes—my fire-souls as
    well—
beautifully made and dancing joyfully in a thousand
    puppet-shows.
And there I left them, happy in the thought
that they would find their way into the rooms
of many, many children.

(Curtain.)

SCENE 4

The same landscape as in the two preceding scenes. The Manager and Romanus pause in their walk.

MANAGER
You are in league with those friends of Hilary
who are involved in spiritual research;
and in you I see an astute and practical man—
one who is always in possession of a sound power of judgement,
whether in the affairs of daily life or in matters of the spirit.
Therefore I do value your opinion.
But how am I to understand what you have just been saying to me?
You think that Strader's friends should stay within the realm of spirit,
and not yet use their clairvoyant powers in the work of practical life.
But shouldn't this apply to Strader too?
Does not the whole disposition of the man
prove that nature-demons always manage to delude him,
whenever he follows up his strong desire to work in the outer world?
The wise pupil of the spirit knows
that he must first strengthen himself inwardly
before he can resist such demons.
But Strader doesn't appear to have developed any awareness of them at all.

ROMANUS
But he's still accompanied by good spiritual powers,
whose task it is to guide those human beings
for whom the gate into the spiritual world remains firmly shut.
These good powers turn away from the pupil,
if he unites with those other kinds of beings

who merely serve his own spiritual mood.
With Strader, I can clearly feel
that nature-demons are still inspiring him
with their *good* forces.

MANAGER And it is only your *feelings* which are convincing you
that good powers are at work in Strader!
My friend, you're asking much of me
for very little in return.
I suppose I too should consult these powers
if I continue working in this place!—
this place, where for so long
it has been my privilege to serve the true spirit of
   work—
so close to the heart of Hilary's father.
It still speaks to me today from the old man's grave,
even now, when his son no longer has an ear for it.
What would this honest, upright man be saying
   today,
if he could see the muddle-headed people
his son is letting into his beloved firm?
How well I came to know this worthy man,
who for ninety years maintained his grip on life.
He it was who taught me the true meaning of work
back in the days when he was still in the thick of
   things,
while his son went slinking off to mystic temples.

ROMANUS Look, my friend, surely you know
how much I myself value the true spirit of work.
The old man, whom you so rightly took as your
   example,
was certainly its loyal servant all his life.
And I too have striven to serve it from my childhood
   to the present day.
And yet, I was also one of those who went slinking
   off to mystic temples.
Whilst there, I faithfully planted into the depths of
   my soul
all that the mystics wished to impart to me.

But when I stepped back into outer life,
I laid aside the temple's mystic mood
and trusted once again in reason and in common-
sense.
I knew that this was the best way
to allow the power of this mood to work into my
practical life.
For you see, I did bring a soul permeated by the
temple back into my work.
And it is best for a soul like this
to be left undisturbed by earthly reason.

MANAGER   And do you really think that Strader's way of
working
is even remotely similar to yours?
In *your* presence, I always feel quite free of the
beings
which work upon me through Strader.
When *he* speaks to me—even when he is mistaken—
I feel how elemental beings are pouring themselves
vigorously into his every word
and into his whole way of being,
revealing things the senses are quite incapable of
perceiving.
And it is just *this* which I find so repelling in the
man.

ROMANUS   What you are saying strikes a deep chord in me.
Ever since I've come to know Strader,
I've experienced his thoughts to be endowed with a
quite special power.
They take hold of me as if they were my very own.
And one day I had to ask myself:
What if it was through *him*—and not myself—
that I've become the man I am today?
And this feeling was soon followed by another:
What if everything which makes me useful in
practical life
and in the service of humanity
were the result of an earlier life on earth?

SCENE 4

MANAGER That is exactly what he makes *me* feel.
The closer one gets to him,
the more powerfully is one gripped by the spiritual force working through him.
If someone as strong as you can be so influenced by him,
then how would *I* protect myself if I joined him in the work?

ROMANUS It will depend solely on yourself
whether or not you can find the right relationship to him.
For my part, I believe that Strader's power over me cannot do me any harm,
because I have formed my own idea
of the way in which he might have once obtained it.

MANAGER Power over you! You mean *he* ... the dreamer ...
obtained power over *you* ... the man of action?

ROMANUS Imagine that in Strader we have an individuality
who in an earlier life on earth
was able to raise himself to rare heights of soul-development,
knowing things that other human beings of his time
could have no inkling of.
If this were true, then thoughts could have once originated in him
that subsequently found their way into the general course of life.
And this is how such people as myself
might have acquired their practical skills in life *today*.
The thoughts which in my youth I took from my environment and made my own
could well have originated from just this individuality.

MANAGER
: And do you really think you're justified
in tracing back those thoughts—of such practical
    value in life today—
to Strader in particular?

ROMANUS
: You know very well I am no dreamer.
I do not blindly spin out ideas about what influences
    our lives.
Nor has it ever been my way
to allow myself to follow trains of thought
that seem at first to offer insight
but only lead to ever deeper obscurity.
I look at Strader quite objectively
and observe just how this man reveals himself
in all his characteristic ways,
in his whole bearing and in his failings too.
And from this it is quite clear to me
that the view I've just expressed to you about his
    special qualities
must be correct.
In my mind's eye I can perceive him now,
as though already many centuries ago he'd once
    stood before me.
I know I am *awake* in this.
And I will not desert Hilary.
What must *will* be.
My friend, why not reconsider your involvement in
    the project?

MANAGER
: It's more important to me now
to consider the things you've just confided in me.

(Manager and Romanus exit. Johannes enters from another direction, deep in thought, and sits on a rock.)

JOHANNES
: I was quite stunned when Capesius described to me
how my inner state of being was revealed to his
    clairvoyant sight.
Thus could a truth be clouded over,

which many years ago was shown to me in all its
    clarity:
that everything which lives in human souls
works on in outer reaches of the spirit.
I knew this long ago ... and yet I could forget it.
When Benedictus first set me on the path to spiritual
    vision,
I was able to perceive in clear picture-form
Capesius and Strader in the spirit,
each at a different age to how I knew them in their
    earthly lives.
I saw how the powerful forms their thinking made
caused waves that spread in circles through the
    universe.
I know all this quite well—
and yet, when it was shown to me by Capesius,
I didn't recognize it.
The 'knowing' part of me was sleeping then.
And I've also known for years
how I was bound up with Capesius in another life on
    earth ...
And in that moment I forgot this too!
How can I hold on to what I know?

JOHANNES' DOUBLE *(voice from the distance)*
'The enchanted weaving
of their own inmost being.'

JOHANNES   'And wakening-dreaming
to souls is revealing
the enchanted weaving
of their own inmost being.'

(While Johannes is speaking, his double approaches him. Johannes does not recognize him, believing him to be the Other Philia.)

Mysterious spirit, you come to me again—
you, who gave to me true counsel.

DOUBLE   Johannes, your awakening will remain illusion,
                until that time when you yourself set free
                the Shadow who, through your guilt,
                is forced to lead a spell-bound life.

JOHANNES   This is the second time you speak these words to me.
                I will be led by them. Show me the way.

DOUBLE   Johannes, what has been lost to you within yourself—
                let it live within the realm of shades.
                But give it light from the light of your own spirit,
                that it no longer need to suffer pain.

JOHANNES   I may well have stunned this shadow-being of mine,
                but I have not yet conquered him.
                He must remain as spell-bound shadow among shadows,
                until I can be one with him again.

DOUBLE   Then give to *me* what you now owe to him:
                the power of love which is driving you to him,
                the hope within your heart which he engendered,
                the source of new life concealed in him,
                the fruits of many long-past lives on earth
                which with his being have now been lost to you—
                give them to me; I'll bring them faithfully to him!

JOHANNES   You know the way to him? Show me!

DOUBLE   Once when you had raised yourself to spirit-spheres,
                I could approach him in the realm of shades.
                But ever since the power of wishes has seduced you
                and your attention has been drawn towards this being,
                my strength must fail me every time I look for him.
                But now, if you will follow my advice,
                I will be able to regain the strength I need.

SCENE 4

JOHANNES I've given you my word that I will follow you.
And now, mysterious spirit, with all my strength of soul,
this resolve I make anew.
Therefore, if you can really find the way to him,
show it to me now in this decisive moment of my life.

DOUBLE I know the way, but cannot lead you there.
All I can do is bring before your eyes of soul
the being you seek so yearningly.

(The Spirit of Johannes' Youth appears.)

SPIRIT OF JOHANNES' YOUTH
I shall remain forever bound
unto the spirit who has opened your soul's eyes,
that when I show myself to you in future times,
in accordance with the Spirit's will,
you will be able then to recognize me clearly.
But this spirit at whose side you see me now,
you must learn to know for what it truly is.

(The Spirit of Johannes' Youth disappears. Only now does the Double become recognizable to Johannes.)

JOHANNES Mysterious spirit? ... No, my other self!

DOUBLE Then follow me; you've given me your word.
It is my duty now to lead you to my Lord.

(The Guardian of the Threshold appears and stands beside the Double.)

GUARDIAN Johannes, if from enchanted worlds of soul
you would set free your shadow-being,
then put to death desires that are enticing you.
The path that you are following will vanish from you,
as long as you are led by your desires.

It leads you to the regions of my threshold
where, in accordance with the will of higher beings,
I must confuse the vision of the soul
when spiritual sight is mingled with desire.
Such sight must first encounter me
before it can attain the pure, clear light of Truth.

(Ahriman enters.)

Your sight too I must hold back,
as long as you approach me with desire.
Your image of me as well is only an illusion,
while illusions born of wish are mingling with your sight,
and peacefulness of spirit as a sheath around your soul
has not yet taken hold of all your being.
Make strong the words of power that you know.
Their spiritual force will conquer your illusion.
And know me—free of your desire,
that you may see the true form of my being.
Then, when you freely turn your gaze to spirit-realms,
I will no longer need to hold you back.

JOHANNES And even *you* appear to me as only an illusion?
You ... who before all other beings in the spiritual world,
I *must* see truly.
What chance have I to know the Truth
if at each step I take, I only find one truth:
that I am treading ever deeper into error!

AHRIMAN Then do not let him get you in a tangle.
He guards his solemn threshold faithfully indeed,
though he stands there in a costume which you've patched up in your mind
from bits and pieces of old melodramas.
As artist, you should never have done him up in such a dreadful style.

| | Later you will surely do it better.
But even this distorted caricature can serve you
　　　now.
And it'll need but little effort on my part
to make you see what you have made of him:
Observe the way he speaks—his tragic tone ...
It's far too sentimental for my taste!
Don't let him get away with it.
And then you'll see
just how much borrowing he's done today—
and from *whom* ...

JOHANNES   And could the *content* of his words be deceiving me
　　　　　　as well?

DOUBLE   Don't ask Ahriman—his chief delight is paradox.

JOHANNES   Then whom should I ask?

DOUBLE   Ask *yourself*.
And I will arm you with my strength,
that in full wakefulness you may find
the place within yourself from where you'll see
that for which you're free of all desire.
Strengthen yourself!

JOHANNES   'The enchanted weaving
of their own inmost being.'
You enchanted weaving of my own inmost being,
show me what it is
for which I'm free of all desire.

(The Guardian disappears. In his place, Benedictus and Maria appear. Ahriman also disappears.)

MARIA   Your image of me as well is only an illusion,
while illusions born of wish are mingling with your
　　　sight.

BENEDICTUS And peacefulness of spirit as a sheath around your soul
has not yet taken hold of all your being.

(Double, Benedictus and Maria disappear.)

JOHANNES *(alone)*
Benedictus and Maria ... as the Guardian!
How is it possible that they appear to me in this form?
I have been with you both for many years ...
Yet still I have to search for you.
For thus commands in all severity
the enchanted weaving of my own inmost being.

(Exit Johannes, stage-right. Strader, Benedictus and Maria enter from the other side.)

STRADER When we met in spiritual communion
before the deep abyss of my own being,
you gave me good advice.
Although at present I do not fully understand it,
it will work on in me
and help me solve the mysteries of my life
that threaten to impede my further progress.
I feel the strength which your work gives to pupils of the spirit.
And therefore I'll certainly be able to give you the help you need,
that the goals of Hilary's project may be achieved.
Capesius will indeed be greatly missed.
The rest of us will never quite be able to fill the gap he leaves.
And yet—what is to be *will* be.

BENEDICTUS What is to be *will* be.
These words correspond to the stage of your development,
but they do not find an echo in the souls of our other friends.

	Johannes is not yet ready to bring the power of the spirit into earthly life.

| | Johannes is not yet ready to bring the power of the spirit into earthly life.
And so he too is now withdrawing from the work.
Through him, a sign of destiny is revealed to us:
from now on, we all must look for other ways... |
|---|---|
| STRADER | And Maria ... and you ... will *you* also not be there? |
| BENEDICTUS | If Maria is truly to find the way
from life in spirit realms back into the physical world,
she must take Johannes with her.
The solemn Guardian, who keeps his watch
over the border between these two worlds,
has willed it must be so.
She cannot give you her support as yet.
And this may serve you as a sign of certainty—
that at present it is not yet possible for you
to truly find the way into the realm of matter. |
| STRADER | So then ... with all my aims ... I stand alone.
Loneliness—was it *you* that came in search of me
that time when I was here with Felix and Capesius? |
| BENEDICTUS | What has now been revealed within our circle
has taught me, in looking at your destiny,
to decipher a certain word in the spirit's light,
which until now had always managed to elude me.
I saw you connected to certain types of beings
which if already now were to play an active role in human affairs,
could only bring evil into the world.
However, they live at present in the human soul as seeds,
in order that they may grow ripe
to serve the earth in future times.
I could observe such seeds within *your* soul.
That you don't know them is a blessing for you.
Through you they'll first come to know themselves. |

	But, at the present time, the door that leads into the realm of matter is still closed to them.
STRADER	Whatever else your words may say, they show me now that loneliness is seeking me. *This* is the power that will truly forge my sword; Maria spoke of this at my abyss.

(Benedictus and Maria draw back a little; to Strader, remaining alone, the Soul of Theodora appears.)

THEODORA'S SOUL	And Theodora will in realms of light engender warmth for you, that your sword of spirit can confront with strength the adversaries of your soul.

(She disappears. Exit Strader. Benedictus and Maria step forward.)

MARIA	My teacher, I have never heard you speak words of destiny in such a way to pupils at Strader's stage upon the Path. Will he really make such rapid progress that the power of these words can be of benefit to him?
BENEDICTUS	It was commanded by the powers of destiny. It had to be.
MARIA	And if your words prove *not* to be of benefit to him, will not their evil consequences fall upon *you* as well?
BENEDICTUS	The consequences will not be evil, but I do not know just *how* they'll manifest in him. Although at present my vision penetrates to realms where such words of counsel can shine into my soul, the *effect* these words will have I cannot see. And if I try ... my vision dies.

SCENE 4

MARIA
: Your vision dies? *Your* vision?
My teacher ... who destroys the steadfast vision of the seer?

BENEDICTUS
: It is Johannes—he flees with it to cosmic distances.
We must pursue. I hear his call.

MARIA
: His call. Out of the furthest reaches of the spirit, it resounds.
And in its sounding streams a distant fear.

BENEDICTUS
: Our friend is calling from the ever-empty fields of ice;
his call is sounding through cosmic distances.

MARIA
: The cold ice burns.
And scorching flames are kindled in my depths—
flames that consume my thinking.

BENEDICTUS
: In your soul's depths, the fire is aflame—
the fire Johannes kindles in the cosmic fields of ice.

MARIA
: The flames are fleeing ... fleeing with my thinking.
And there ... at the cosmic shoreline of the soul ...
a raging battle! ... My own thinking fights ...
amidst the torrents of the void ... with cold spiritual light.
My thinking wavers; ... cold light ...
striking out hot darkness from my thinking.

  What rises now out of the darkness of the heat?
My Self in red flames storms into the light ...
the cold light ... storms into the cosmic fields of ice!

  (Curtain.)

SCENE 5

The Spiritual World. The scene is set in floods of colour: above, reddish going into fiery-red; below, blue going into a dark-blue and violet, with a symbolically represented earth-sphere.

The figures appear as though blending in with the colours of the whole scene. Stage-left—the group of gnomes from Scene 2. In front of them—Hilary. At the very front—the soul-forces. Behind Hilary, somewhat raised—Ahriman. Downstage, far stage-right—the soul of Felix Balde. Raised behind him and to his left—Lucifer. Stage-left—Strader's soul, across from the soul of Felix Balde.

FELIX BALDE'S SOUL

    (Appearing as a penitent, but wearing a light-violet robe with a gold belt.)

    Thanks be to you, wise Spirit who governs worlds.
    You have released me from dark solitude.
    Your words awaken me to life and work.
    I shall make use of what you give to worlds,
    on which I then may muse when my *own* world
    you let sink down in deep oblivion.
    You bear into these worlds upon your streaming
    what in creating forms for me new power.

LUCIFER

    (Bluish-green, shining under-garment; brightly-shining, reddish outer-garment in the form of a cloak that extends into winglike shapes. Above him, instead of an aura, a dark-red headdress in the form of a mitre with wings. On his right wing is a blue, swordlike shape; his left wing supports a yellow, planet-like sphere.)

    My servant, such activity as yours
    demands the hour of Sun which we have entered.
    The earth-star now receives but little light.
    This is the hour when souls that have *your* gifts
    can profit most by working on themselves.

From out my fount of light, I brightly stream to you
seed-force of self-awareness.
Receive it now and make your ego strong.
It will in earth-existence bloom for you.
And there your soul will seek the shining blossoms,
delighting in the feeling of itself,
when it in pleasure dwells on its desires.

FELIX BALDE'S SOUL *(looking at the group of gnomes)*
There far away a bright existence fades.
It floats in misty forms towards the depths;
in floating it is longing to find weight.

HILARY'S SOUL

(In the form of a steel-blue grey elemental being, but modified to resemble a man—the head less bowed and the limbs more human.)

This mist of longing is the earthly star
reflected back to regions of the spirit—
that star for which in *this* world you prepare
a life in thought from substances of soul.
To you it seems a web of passing mist;
but in itself it is a world of beings,
who feel themselves possessed of weight of soul.
They work on earth with cosmic intellect
in ancient fiery depths which thirst for form.

FELIX BALDE'S SOUL
I do not want their weight to burden me.
It gives resistance to my wish to float.

AHRIMAN   Fine words, indeed! I'll grab them quickly,
that I may keep them for myself unspoiled.
You cannot further foster them yourself,
and you would hate to hear them on the earth.

STRADER'S SOUL

(Only his head is visible, having a yellow-green aura with red and orange stars.)

Words I am hearing—sounding, echoing;
words full of meaning, yet their sounding dies away.
Their echoing is seized by lust for life.
In which direction will it choose to turn?

OTHER PHILIA

(Like a copy of Lucifer, but lacking the radiance of his garments. Instead of the sword, a kind of dagger. And instead of the sphere, a red ball like a fruit.)

In yearning to have weight, it travels onward
to there where bright existence fades away
and enters depths as misty images.
If you will guard its meaning in your realm,
then I will bring you strength within the mist,
which you will find again upon the earth.

PHILIA

(Angelic form, yellow going into white with bright violet wings, of a lighter shade than those which Maria has later. All three are close to Strader's soul.)

I'll tend the beings of the mist for you,
that they unknown to you may guide your will;
and I'll entrust your will to cosmic light,
where their creative work will warm your being.

ASTRID

(Angelic form, light-violet robe with blue wings.)

Bright joyfulness of starry life I'll stream
unto these beings, that they may give it form;
your earthly body they'll make strong for you,
though far from knowledge, close to powers of
    heart.

LUNA

(Slender angelic form, blue-red robe with orange wings.)

Substance of weight which they create with toil—
within your body I'll conceal from you;
that you in thinking turn it not to evil
and thereby raise a tempest on the earth.

SCENE 5

STRADER'S SOUL

  The three were speaking radiant, sun-filled words.
  They work and weave in everything I see,
  and countless forms they fashion all around.
  A longing stirs to shape them into one
  possessed of strength of soul and filled with
    meaning.
  Awaken for me, kingly power of Sun,
  that I may dim you down through the resistance
  my wishes carry from the lunar sphere.
  There rises now a golden glow of warmth
  and silver light that sparkles with cold thoughts.
  Gleam on, you wishful urge of Mercury—
  unite for me divided world-existence.

  And now I clearly feel how once again
  an image has been partly formed for me,
  which I am called to work on further here
  out of the spiritual forces of the world.

  (Exit Ahriman.)

CAPESIUS' SOUL

  (Appearing at Strader's first lines; only his head is visible, which has a blue aura with red and yellow stars.)

  On distant shores of soul, an image rises.
  It has not touched my being since the time
  that I last wrenched myself from earthly life.
  It radiates a gentle, healing grace.
  The warming glow of wisdom streams from it;
  and it bestows a clarifying light.
  If I could weave it into oneness with myself,
  I would be granted that for which I thirst.
  And yet I cannot find the active power
  to make this image live within my sphere.

LUNA

  Now feel what two earth-lives have given you.
  In ancient times, the first one flowed on by
  in solemn transformation, while the second

you lived through greatly darkened by ambition.
Imbue the later life with powers of grace
arising from the former. Then for you
the souls of fire from Jupiter will rise
and be revealed within your sphere of sight.
By wisdom you'll be strengthened. And that image,
which still appears on far shores of your soul,
will then be able to move close to you.

CAPESIUS' SOUL

Do I then owe a *debt* unto this soul,
which now prepares itself for earthly life,
that I am *warned* by its reflected image?

ASTRID

You do indeed. But it does not yet ask
atonement from you in your next earth-life.
Its image will endow your thought with strength,
that you on earth can find the one who now
reveals to you his future earthly life.

OTHER PHILIA

The image may come nearer to you still,
but cannot penetrate your sphere of being.
Hold back therefore the urge it streams to you,
that you can find yourself on earth once more
before it flows into your inmost being.

CAPESIUS' SOUL

I feel what I will one day owe this image,
if I can bring it closer to myself,
whilst holding my own ground apart from it.
Appearing now from Philia's realm I see,
revealed to me as thoughts in picture-form,
the strength that I shall draw through its approach.

PHILIA

When Saturn's rays of many-coloured light
soon shine into your soul, use well the hour!
The image of the one akin to you
will then be able to plant roots of thought
within your soul. These shall reveal to you

SCENE 5

>
> the meaning of the history of the earth,
> when this star bears and nurtures you once more.

CAPESIUS' SOUL
> The guidance that you give shall serve me well,
> when Saturn soon will shine its light on me.

LUCIFER
> I will awaken in these Sun-filled souls
> the spectacle of worlds whose light brings pain.
> This I will do before they leave the Sun
> with forces for their coming life on earth.
> Through pain they must be fructified with doubt.
> And I will summon up those spheres of soul,
> which they are not empowered to behold.

(Benedictus' and Maria's souls appear mid-stage—the former as a figure whose dress represents in microcosm the entire visual scene. Around his head, an aura of red, yellow and blue. The blue blends into the blue-green of his robe, which widens at the bottom. Maria as an angelic figure—yellow blending into gold, without feet and with light-violet wings.)

BENEDICTUS' SOUL
> Your heavy spheres, made dense with weight of earth,
> are pressing down upon my cosmic sphere.
> Should your self-seeking be allowed to grow,
> then you would find that in this life of spirit
> my Sun-filled being could no more shine in you.

MARIA'S SOUL
> He was unknown to you when last you wore
> a garment woven out of earthly substances;
> and yet the radiant Sun-Word's power, with which
> in ancient times on earth he nurtured you,
> continues to bear fruit within your souls.
> Then know the deepest impulse of your being
> and you will strongly feel that he is near.

Felix Balde's Soul

> From spheres unknown to me there sound forth
>   words;
> and yet their tones create no bright existence.
> And so they are not fully real to me.

Strader's Soul

> I see a shining being on spirit-shores;
> but it is silent, though I struggle hard
> to hear the meaning of its radiant power.

Felicia Balde's Soul

> *(The figure of a penitent—yellow-orange robe, silver belt—appearing close to Maria.)*
>
> You souls, whom Lucifer has summoned here—
> the penitent can hear your words as sound,
> and yet, only the *Sun-Word* shines for him;
> its dazzling light is drowning out your speech.
> The other can behold your starry light;
> the starry script, though, is unknown to him.

Capesius' Soul

> The starry script ... these words awaken thoughts;
> they carry them to me on waves of soul—
> the thoughts that in a long-past life on earth
> were once revealed to me in all their splendour.
> They shine ... but in becoming ... they are
>   vanishing,
> and round me spread oblivion's dark shadows.

Guardian

> *(Symbolically represented in the form of an angel, stepping towards and speaking to the souls of Benedictus and Maria.)*
>
> You souls, who now at Lucifer's command,
> approach the circle of these other souls—
> in this place you are under my dominion.
> The souls whom you are seeking, seek you too.
> But at this cosmic hour it is not right

that in their spheres they touch you with their
    thoughts.
Take heed you do not penetrate their spheres,
for this would greatly harm both you and them.
And I would have to dim the starry light
and banish you from them to other realms
for cosmic ages ...

(Slow curtain.)

SCENE 6

The Spiritual World, as in the preceding scene. The lighting warm and differentiated, but not too bright. Stage-right—the group of sylphs. In front—Philia, Astrid and Luna. Mid-stage-left—the soul of Capesius, close to those of Romanus, Torquatus and Bellicosus.

CAPESIUS' SOUL
>The image shown me at the hour of Sun,
>which radiated grace and gentle healing,
>is working on me still, whilst even now
>a different kind of wisdom floods this realm
>with shining rays of many-coloured light.
>Yet still more power streams from the image now;
>it bids me draw from it for future lives
>what once upon the earth was given to me
>by him, who in this image shows himself
>with deep significance unto my sphere.
>And yet, I find no active stream of feeling
>to lead me to this soul.

ROMANUS' SOUL
>*(A figure visible from the hips up, with mighty red wings that extend around his head into a red aura, blending to blue at its rim.)*
>
>>Arouse in you
>the image of the Jew, who from all sides
>heard only hate and mockery, and yet
>gave loyal service to that brotherhood
>to which in former times you once belonged.

CAPESIUS' SOUL
>Thought-images are dawning, and they seek
>with all their strength to take a hold of me.
>From out the surging waves of soul there rises
>the image of the one I knew as Simon.

But now another soul is joining him—
a penitent—keep him away from me!

(Felix Balde's soul appears.)

ROMANUS' SOUL
> Only at the cosmic hour of Sun
> is he enabled to perform his work.
> In loneliness he wanders, wrapped in darkness,
> when Saturn shines its light upon this realm.

CAPESIUS' SOUL
> This penitent—how he confuses me!
> What streams out of his soul is burning me
> and penetrating deep into my sheaths.
> This is what happens when a soul is able
> to see into another's deepest being.

FELIX BALDE'S SOUL *(in a dull, muffled voice)*
> 'Dear Kean, you have always proved most loyal...'

CAPESIUS' SOUL
> My self... my very words... spoken by him...
> They echo on, resounding through this realm.
> This is the soul whom I will have to seek.
> He knows me well; through him I'll find myself.

(Capesius' soul disappears. From stage-right the Other Philia and Theodora's soul appear, followed by Felicia Balde's soul.)

ROMANUS' SOUL
> Two souls are drawing near the penitent.
> Ahead of them there steps that graceful spirit,
> whom souls through love acquire to be their guide.
> From one soul streams a gently-warming light.
> It flows towards the other, who herself
> appears to us in robes of penitence.
> The image radiates a glow of beauty,
> which lives as wisdom in this spirit-realm.

TORQUATUS' SOUL
> *(A figure visible down to the breast, with blue aura and green wings.)*

> You see a mirrored image of the longing,
> which I let stream to you from my soul's sheaths
> in true and loving spirit-brotherhood.
> For primal powers of destiny ordain
> that through me gentleness is born in you.
> In such ways souls in spirit serve each other.
> You on your own could never find the way
> to join unto your hard, unyielding nature
> the living gift of human sympathy.

BELLICOSUS' SOUL
> *(A figure, like Torquatus, visible down to the breast, but with a blue-violet aura and blue-green wings.)*

> Grow strong in spirit-hearing, for there speaks
> the soul whose streaming light is gentleness.
> This light, which fills the world with grace and
>   blessing,
> is here, by Saturn's glow, released for souls.

THEODORA'S SOUL
> *(Angelic form, white with yellow wings and blue-yellow aura.)*

> True sister of the spirit, stream to him
> your soul's pure love in gently glowing light.
> For loneliness consumes him with its flames
> and you shall mitigate their fiercest power.
> Direct to him the thoughts that radiate
> from shadow-souls, who mingle over there;
> they gather here the forces which they need
> to make their starry bodies gleam with life,
> that from their glimmering light's creative power
> the sensing of becoming and of growth
> be strengthened on the earth for human souls.

FELICIA BALDE'S SOUL

>You spirit penitent, now feel me near;
>receive, Sun-soul, the strength of stars from me.
>Until you wrest your spirit-sheaths away
>from Lucifer's domain, I'll be your guide.
>Throughout your solitude I'll bring to you
>the forces that I'll gather from all worlds,
>as, wandering, I pass from star to star.

THEODORA'S SOUL

>Past earthly thoughts are rising, glimmering—
>and there on shores of soul ... a human form ...
>appearing as on earth ... approaching me.
>It echoes words which I have heard before:
>'From God the human soul once had its birth;
>in death it can descend to depths of being;
>in time it will from death set free the spirit.'

>*(During the last speech, Lucifer and Johannes' soul have appeared.)*

OTHER PHILIA

>This sounding human form is bearing here
>the active force of purest brother-love,
>which you achieved in loyalty on earth.
>I'll change it into power of soul for you.
>The light of shadow-beings will receive
>the word, which I direct towards your soul.
>In earthly life they will inspire in you
>what they have mused on in eternity.
>And you, the penitent in spirit-realms,
>direct your steps of soul towards the stars.
>For nature-spirits long to take your work,
>that they may kindle fantasy in souls,
>and so create the wings for earthly life.

FELICIA BALDE'S SOUL

>I'll follow you—my sister of the soul,
>my Philia, who forms and fashions love—
>from star to star, from spirit unto spirit.

I'll follow you to starry worlds afar
and bear your word to many a circling sphere.
And in this work I'll form myself as well
towards my future pilgrimage on earth.

(Felix Balde's soul, led by Felicia Balde's soul, disappears slowly. Theodora remains for a while motionless, gazing at Johannes' soul; then she too disappears, as does Johannes' soul with Lucifer.)

ROMANUS' SOUL

That we have witnessed in this spirit-sphere
the word of love join with the word of deed—
this will give strength to seeds within our souls,
which we shall need in later lives on earth.

(The souls of Romanus, Torquatus and Bellicosus disappear. The souls of Benedictus and Maria appear beside the Guardian of the Threshold.)

GUARDIAN

Awaken to your cosmic midnight hour!
I hold you in the wise and ancient glow
that Saturn turns on you, till through its power
your sheaths of soul, illuminating you,
reveal in greater wakefulness their colours.

MARIA'S SOUL

Awake ... within the cosmic midnight hour?
It was the lunar hour ... The Sun proclaimed
the solemn word of destiny: Those souls,
who are awake within the midnight hour,
behold in sudden flashes of bright lightning
the things that in the course of time *must be*.
Such insights die away as they are known,
and, dying, form the script of destiny
eternally engraved in human souls.
These souls hear words of thunder, dully rolling,
which rumble and resound in depths of worlds
and threaten all illusion as they roll.

SCENE 6

(Lucifer and Johannes' soul appear again.)

BENEDICTUS' SOUL

    From ever-empty fields of ice, there sounds
    an urgent call of destiny to us.
    We'll reach the spirit-sphere of our good friend
    when we awaken to the midnight hour.

MARIA'S SOUL

    The flames approach ... approaching with my
        thinking ...
    there, from the cosmic shoreline of my soul.
    A fiery battle looms ... My thinking fights
    against the scorching thoughts of Lucifer ...
    My thoughts are battling in another's soul ...
    From darkest cold there streams a fiery light ...
    a fiery light of soul—it flames like lightning!—
    the light of soul ... in cosmic fields of ice.

LUCIFER   Behold the light, my fiery cosmic light;
    and see the lightning, which your thinking strikes
    from realms where power of Lucifer holds sway.
    While you experience now your midnight hour,
    I bring into your field of sight that soul
    to whom for ages long you have been bound.
    If you would once again draw near to it,
    you must in future change your ways of seeking.

    And you—the soul whom I have guided here—
    use well the power of light that Saturn streams
    upon her at her cosmic midnight hour.

JOHANNES' SOUL

    *(Like an angel in form, rose-red, without feet and with
    blue-red wings.)*

    I sense that souls are near, but I lack strength
    to feel their light as power of being in me.
    However near they are, the thoughts they form
    appear to me as shining from afar.

How can I raise them into spirit-vision?

PHILIA You will perceive them if you quickly grasp
what they illuminate in cosmic light.
But in perceiving, seize the moment's grace:
the light once kindled swiftly disappears.

JOHANNES' SOUL
The words the teacher's soul speaks to his pupil—
that pupil's soul, so close, so dear to me—
shall fill the circle of my soul with light.

BENEDICTUS' SOUL
Create, in this the Spirit's midnight hour,
your powers of will, which once again you'll feel
when forces of the earth renew your form.
Your word's light-power shall shine upon your
    friend.

MARIA'S SOUL
So let my word gain strength in cosmic light—
my word entrusted at the midnight hour
unto the soul brought here by Lucifer.
I will behold—and in beholding speak—
what in my depths of being I cherish most,
that in this soul it may be formed to tone—
a tone which on the earth he then may feel
and lovingly let live within his being.
What is it that I see now in my depths?
A fiery script is shining forth to me;
my love is flaming out towards my teacher—
the one who, both on earth and in the spirit,
has guided me throughout long tides of time,
who always found me when in urgent prayer
I sought him at the times of greatest danger,
who came to me as well when he himself
dwelt only in the spirit. Shining bright
this love appears to me. You word of love,
sound forth from me unto this other soul!

But with this word of love what flames are kindled?
They gently glow; and glowing, radiate
a deep solemnity. Now full of grace
there flickers through the ethers—wisdom's
    lightning.
And blessedness, poured forth in joyful weaving,
fills all the wide horizons of my soul.
Eternal time, hear this my ardent prayer—
flow mightily into this blessedness;
and let the teacher, let the other soul
abide with me within you, filled with peace.

GUARDIAN   May lightning vanish into nothingness—
the lightning that illumines *what must be*
to souls who waken in the cosmic North.
And may the thunder lose its warning roll,
which rumbles through the cosmic midnight hour.
Astrid—to you I give this strict command:
Safeguard the raging tempest of this soul,
until once more the cosmic midnight hour
finds her awake within the stream of time.
When then she stands before herself in spirit,
she'll see herself in ancient times transformed.
She'll learn how wings for spiritual ascent
are strengthened also if the soul should fall.
The wish to fall should never tempt the soul;
but from each fall it must acquire new wisdom.

ASTRID   I'll guard the power of lightning and of thunder,
preserving it within the being of worlds,
till Saturn's light shall shine on her once more.

MARIA'S SOUL
    Abiding, I feel blessedness of stars,
which I may enter in the stream of time.
Upheld by grace, I'll live creatively
with my friend's soul so closely bound to mine.

LUNA   In spirit-realms I'll guard what you create,
that it may ripen for you on the earth.

JOHANNES' SOUL

>Within the circle of my soul ... a star!
>Its light is blessedness ... it shines forth grace ...
>A star of soul in cosmic ether ... gliding ...
>
>But there ... with feeble light ... another star.
>Though faint its sound, I wish to hear it speak.

(With these last words, the Spirit of Johannes' Youth appears—like an angel with a silvery light.)

SPIRIT OF JOHANNES' YOUTH

>With life I feed the substance of your wishes.
>Into your youthful, glowing aims, I'll breathe
>a shining strength, when worlds are calling you,
>in which I joyfully can be your guide.
>If you forget that I am part of you,
>I'll lose my being—a sacrifice to shadows.
>You blossom of my life, do not abandon me!

LUCIFER

>Abandon you? This he will never do.
>For I can see within his being's depths
>desires for light that never will submit
>unto the guidance of that other soul.
>When these desires, with all their shining splendour,
>take stronger grip within his depths of soul,
>then he'll no longer wish to waste their fruits
>in realms where love holds sway bereft of beauty.

(Slow curtain.)

SCENE 7

A temple in Egyptian style—a place of initiation in the third cultural epoch of the earth. On stage—the Hierophant, the Temple Warden and the Mystic.

In this and in the following scene, the name of the individuality in his or her modern incarnation is given the first time they speak.

HIEROPHANT *(Capesius)*
    Has everything been properly prepared, my Temple Warden,
    that this initiation may rightly serve
    both humanity and the gods?

TEMPLE WARDEN *(Felix)*
    As far as we are able to foresee,
    all things have been *well* prepared;
    for many days the Temple has been filled
    with consecrated air.

HIEROPHANT My Mystic, the priest who on this day
    will be initiated into hidden wisdom
    is chosen as advisor to the King.
    Did you structure his trial in such a way
    that he has not succumbed to other-worldliness?
    A counsellor devoted only to the spirit
    would be damaging to us.

MYSTIC *(Felicia)*
    The trial was conducted in accordance with correct procedure;
    the Masters gave it their complete approval.
    However, it seems to me
    the pupil has but little care for earthly matters.
    His soul strives only for the spirit;
    he is preoccupied with self-development alone.
    I've often seen him in a state of trance.

                In fact, it's not too much to say
                that he quite *revels* in the feeling of spiritual
                    communion.

HIEROPHANT   Have you often seen him in this state?

MYSTIC   Indeed, he has appeared like this quite frequently.
             Surely he'd be better suited as servant in the
                 Temple,
             than as advisor to the King.

HIEROPHANT   That is enough. Now go about your duty.
             And see that this initiation shall succeed.

                (Exit Mystic.)

                But you, my Temple Warden, hear me further.
                You know how much I value your mystic gift of
                    insight.
                To me, you stand much higher with your wisdom
                than your position in the Temple indicates.
                And I have often turned to you
                to test the truth of my own spiritual perception.
                Therefore I ask you now—
                how much confidence do you really have
                in this pupil's spiritual maturity?

TEMPLE WARDEN
                Who cares about what I think?
                My voice counts for nothing here.

HIEROPHANT   For me, it always counts.
             Today you will once more stand by me.
             We must accompany this initiation with our eyes of
                 soul wide open.
             And should the pupil show even the slightest sign
             that he is falling short of our high goals,
             then I'll prevent him from becoming an advisor.

TEMPLE WARDEN
>What is it about this pupil that could come to light
during his initiation?

HIEROPHANT I know he is not worthy of the honour
that the servants of the Temple put upon him.
His inner disposition is well known to me.
True mysticism stirs within the human heart
when from above the spirit's light
rains down in grace upon the soul
and draws it to itself.
But this is not what lives within *his* heart.
Passion still surges strongly through his veins;
sensual urges he has not yet stilled.
For this, I do not blame the will of the gods,
whose light, within the stream of earthly life,
wisely shines even into the darkness of desire.
But when desire conceals itself
behind a mask of reverent devotion,
it causes thought to err and corrupts the will.
The light that weaves in spirit-worlds
cannot penetrate such souls as these,
for they are shrouded in a mystic fog.

TEMPLE WARDEN
>My Hierophant, your judgement is severe
of one so young and inexperienced.
As yet, he cannot know himself.
All he can do is tread the path
the Masters have prescribed for him.

HIEROPHANT I do not judge the man; I judge the deed,
which in this sacred place will be performed.
The sacrificial work that we fulfil
is of significance not for ourselves alone:
within our sacred act, world-destiny
streams as a mighty force through word and deed.
What here in ritual we enact on earth,
becomes in spirit-realms eternal life.

But now, my Temple Warden, go about your work.
You will yourself find out
how best you can assist me during the initiation.

(Exit Temple Warden.)

If in the hours to come there should escape
impure emotions from this young pupil's heart—
emotions that would stream into our sacred act
and rise as images into the realm of gods—
then *he* would not be to blame.
Should such an act of sacrilege take place,
from which into human life destructive force would
    flow,
the guilty ones would be the *Masters*.
Can they still see how in our ritual act
mysteriously a hidden power
fills with spirit each word and deed?
And how this power can also work destructively
when personal emotion mingles with it?
Instead of this young pupil
offering himself consciously to the spirit,
his Masters drag him as a sacrifice to the altar,
where he is forced to yield unconsciously
what lives within his soul.
But if he could sustain his soul in consciousness,
he'd surely find the way
to direct his sacrifice quite differently.
Within our circle, only the Chief Hierophant
is fully aware of what as hidden power
lives within this ritual's form.
But in accordance with the oath of his high office,
he is as silent as the grave.
And when I try to speak to the others
about the seriousness of our work,
they simply do not understand.

So here I stand alone in my dilemma.
And when I feel the deep significance of this
    Temple,

it all oppresses me.
Loneliness—here in this solemn and sacred place,
I have come to know you deeply.
Why am I alone here?
My soul is compelled to ask—but the Spirit,
when will it give me answer?

(Slow curtain.)

SCENE 8

The same as in the preceding scene, but masked at first by a curtain. In front—an Egyptian woman.

EGYPTIAN WOMAN *(Johannes)*
>This is the hour in which he offers up his being
>to age-old service in the Mysteries—
>the hour that tears him from my side forever.
>Out of the light-filled heights to which he turns,
>a ray of death descends upon my soul.
>Without him, what is there on this earth for me
>but grief, renunciation, suffering ... and death.
>
>But in this hour when he abandons me,
>I will remain close to the sacred place
>at which he dedicates himself unto the spirit.
>And if I may not see it with my eyes—
>how he is wrenched away from earth—
>perhaps the revelation of a dream
>will let me linger with him yet a while in spirit.
>
>*The curtain opens revealing everything made ready for the initiation of the Neophyte. In the middle—an altar. On one side—the Chief Hierophant. On the other—the Keeper of the Word. Somewhat in front of the altar—the Guardian of the Seals. In front and to one side of it—the Representatives of the Earth and Air elements. Close to the Chief Hierophant—the Hierophant. On the other side—the Representatives of the Fire and Water elements. Downstage—Philia, Astrid, Luna and the Other Philia. In front of them—Lucifer and Ahriman in the form of two sphinxes, Lucifer with the angel emphasized, Ahriman with the bull emphasized. Four other priests stand in front.*
>
>*A period of silence. Then the Neophyte is led in from*

stage-right by the Temple Warden and the Mystic. They direct him to the altar and remain close.

TEMPLE WARDEN *(Felix)*
>From out that web of semblance you call 'world',
>while you in error's darkness are ensnared,
>the Mystic has now led you to this place.
>From Being and Nothingness the world was made—
>the world whose semblance wove itself for you.
>Semblance is good when seen in truth by Being;
>but you have dreamt it in your semblance life.
>And semblance known by semblance falls away.
>You semblance of a semblance—know yourself!

MYSTIC *(Felicia)*
>Thus speaks the one who guards this Temple's door;
>feel in yourself the full weight of his word.

REPRESENTATIVE OF THE EARTH ELEMENT *(Romanus)*
>In heavy weight of earth-existence grasp
>the semblance of your being fearlessly,
>that you may sink into the cosmic depths.
>In cosmic depths now seek for Being in darkness.
>And bind unto your semblance what you find:
>in weight you will be granted your own being.

KEEPER OF THE WORD *(Hilary)*
>You'll know to where we're leading you in sinking,
>when you have followed what his word commands.
>We forge for you the form of your own being.
>Know then our work; or else you will dissolve
>as semblance into cosmic nothingness.

MYSTIC
>Thus speaks the one who guards this Temple's words;
>feel in yourself his word's resounding weight.

REPRESENTATIVE OF THE AIR ELEMENT *(Magnus Bellicosus)*
    From heavy weight of earth-existence flee;
    your selfhood's being is deadened in its sinking.
    With airy lightness swiftly fly away.
    In cosmic widths now seek for Being in brightness.
    And bind unto your semblance what you find:
    in flight you will be granted your own being.

KEEPER OF THE WORD
    You'll know to where we're leading you in flying,
    when you have followed what his word commands.
    We lighten up the life of your own being.
    Know then our work; or else you will dissolve
    as semblance into cosmic weight.

MYSTIC   Thus speaks the one who guards this Temple's words;
    feel in yourself his wing'd word's power of flight.

CHIEF HIEROPHANT *(Benedictus)*
    My son, upon the royal road to wisdom
    you shall obey in truth these priests' commands.
    You cannot see the answer in yourself,
    for error's darkness blinds and binds you still,
    and folly strives in you for distant worlds.
    So look into this flame—it is to you

    (the sacred fire flares up from the altar in bright tongues of flame)

    still closer than the life of your own being—
    and read the answer shown to you by fire.

MYSTIC   Thus speaks the one who leads this Temple's rites;
    feel in yourself their consecrating power.

REPRESENTATIVE OF THE FIRE ELEMENT *(Strader)*
    The error of your selfhood—let it burn
    within the fire enkindled in this rite.
    And with your error be *yourself* consumed.

In cosmic fire now seek your being as flame.
And bind unto your semblance what you find:
in burning you'll be granted your own being.

GUARDIAN OF THE SEALS *(Theodora)*
You'll know why we are forming you as flame,
when you have followed what his word commands.
We purify the form of your own being.
Know then our work; or else you will be lost
in formlessness amidst the cosmic water.

MYSTIC   Thus speaks the one who guards this Temple's seal;
feel in yourself the power of wisdom's light.

REPRESENTATIVE OF THE WATER ELEMENT *(Torquatus)*
The flaming force of fiery worlds restrain;
it would consume the strength of your own being.
The only way that semblance becomes Being
is when the beating waves of cosmic water
can fill you with the music of the spheres.
In cosmic water seek your being as wave.
And bind unto your semblance what you find:
in surging you'll be granted your own being.

GUARDIAN OF THE SEALS
You'll know why we are forming you as wave,
when you have followed what his word commands.
We mould for you the form of your own being.
Know then our work; or else you will be lost
in formlessness amidst the cosmic fire.

CHIEF HIEROPHANT
My son, with all your strongest powers of will,
you shall obey these priests' commands as well.
You cannot see the answer in yourself—
in cowardly fear your power is frozen still;
in weakness you now fail to form the wave
that lets you sound and ring throughout the spheres.
So listen to the forces of your soul,
and recognize your own voice in their speech.

PHILIA	In fire be cleansed; as wave in cosmic ocean
	now lose yourself within the sounding spheres.

ASTRID Within the sounding spheres now form yourself;
in cosmic distances fly light as air.

LUNA In world-foundations sink with weight of earth;
draw courage from the depths to live as self.

OTHER PHILIA
Release yourself from personal existence;
unite yourself with elemental power.

MYSTIC Thus speaks within the Temple *your own soul*;
feel in this place the guidance of its forces.

CHIEF HIEROPHANT
My brother, sound the depths of this young soul,
whom we are bound to lead on wisdom's path.
Disclose to us your vision of its state.

HIEROPHANT *(Capesius)*
All goes just as our holy rite ordains.
The soul has quite forgotten what it was.
Through contradictions of the elements
the web of semblance has been purged from it.
This web lives on in elemental strife;
the soul, though, has preserved its core alone.
What lives within this core it now must read
in cosmic Word arising from the flame.

CHIEF HIEROPHANT
Then read, O human soul, what from the flame
in cosmic Word your inmost core proclaims.

(A lengthy pause. It grows dark—only the flame and the indistinct outlines of the priests remain visible.)

And now awaken from your cosmic vision.
Reveal what you have read within the Word.

SCENE 8

(The Neophyte is silent. The Chief Hierophant continues, alarmed.)

He's silent! Has the vision vanished? Speak!

NEOPHYTE *(Maria)*
> Obedient to your ritual's strict command,
> I sank into the being of the flame
> and waited for the sounding of the Word.

(The assembled priests, with the exception of the Hierophant, reveal during the speech of the Neophyte a growing alarm.)

> I felt how from the leaden weight of earth
> I could, with airy lightness, free myself.
> Then, lovingly received by cosmic fire,
> I felt myself in flowing spirit-waves.
> I saw my earthly body from without,
> appearing to me as another being.
> Upborne upon the streaming waves of bliss,
> I felt myself in realms of spirit-light.
> And yet, in gazing on my earthly form,
> I could but long for what felt part of me.
> Upon it streamed the light of higher worlds.
> And, like a host of shining butterflies,
> there hovered round it beings who tend its life.
> Their shimmering light was mirrored by my body
> in sparkling play of colour all around,
> which gleamed close by, more gently glowed afar,
> and faded in the distances of space.
> And then within me grew the deepest longing—
> that heavy weight of earth would pull me down
> and sink me in my body, where once more
> I joyfully could bathe in warmth of life.
> And gladly diving down into my body
> I heard your urgent summons to awake.

CHIEF HIEROPHANT *(greatly disturbed, to the agitated participants)*
> That is no spiritual vision!
> Mere earthly feeling
> has escaped from the soul of this neophyte
> and risen up as offering into the higher realms of
>   light!
> It is an outrage to the gods, a deed of sacrilege!

KEEPER OF THE WORD *(angrily, to the Hierophant)*
> This would never have been possible
> if you had only carried out the duty of your office
> in accordance with our ancient customs!

HIEROPHANT I did what at this hour of sacrifice
> was laid on me as duty by the gods.
> I stopped myself from thinking on the word
> which ancient codes have handed down to me—
> the word which, streaming out from my own
>   thought,
> should then have worked upon the neophyte.
> And thus, his words did not come from another—
> the voice of his *own* being you here have heard.
> The truth has conquered. You may punish me.
> I *had* to do what fills you with such fear.
> I feel the times approach, that will set free
> the single self from life within the group,
> thus liberating independent thought.
> This neophyte may now escape your path,
> but later lives on earth will see to it
> that he is led upon the mystic way
> intended for him by world-destiny.

PRIESTS *(in a babble of voices)*
> Monstrous sacrilege!
> Outrage!
> This demands atonement!
> Punish the blasphemy!

(The two sphinxes begin to speak with the voices of Ahriman and Lucifer. Beforehand, they were as

statues—motionless. They are heard only by the Hierophant, the Chief Hierophant and the Neophyte. The others remain in a state of high excitement through what has already happened.)

AHRIMAN AS SPHINX

> What here unlawfully has sought for light
> I must ensnare and seize for my domain.
> In darkness I must further nurture it.
> And thus in spirit it shall form the power,
> which one day, sensing when the time is ripe,
> will work in human life with good effect.
> But till this power is formed, *my* work is served
> by all that in this holy ritual here
> has been made manifest as weight of earth.

LUCIFER AS SPHINX

> What here as spirit-wish delights in semblance
> I will now carry off to my domain.
> As semblance it shall shine with joy in light
> and give itself in spirit unto beauty—
> such beauty as it cannot reach at present,
> because earth's heavy burden weighs it down.
> In beauty, semblance is transformed to Being;
> and as the light that here flies free, descending,
> it will in future be the light of earth.

CHIEF HIEROPHANT

> The sphinxes speak! Since first these rites were formed,
> they've been no more than graven images.
> The spirit has seized hold of lifeless matter.
> O, Destiny—you sound as cosmic Word!

(The other priests, with the exception of the Hierophant and the Neophyte, are shocked by the Chief Hierophant's words.)

HIEROPHANT *(to the Chief Hierophant)*
>The sacrificial work that we fulfil
>is of significance not for ourselves alone:
>within our sacred act, world-destiny
>streams as a mighty force through word and deed.

(Curtain, while the excitement is at its pitch.)

SCENE 9

A small room, like a study, in the house of Hilary. A mood of seriousness. Maria alone in meditation.

MARIA
A star of soul ... there at the spirit-shore;
it is approaching me ... approaching me in light.
With my own Self it comes ... As it draws near ...
its light grows still more powerful ... more peaceful too.
You star within my spiritual horizon,
what is your shining presence bringing me?

(Astrid appears.)

ASTRID
Perceive what I bestow on you.
Out of the battle between light and dark,
I stole your thinking's power.
And from the cosmic midnight's hour of wakening,
I faithfully return it to you now,
here in your earthly form.

MARIA
Astrid, until now you have always appeared to me
but as a luminous soul-shadow.
What has transformed you into this bright spirit-star?

ASTRID
I have preserved the lightning and the thunder's power,
safeguarding it for you in depths of soul.
But now you can perceive it consciously—
remembering the cosmic midnight hour.

MARIA
The cosmic midnight hour ...
before the husk of this earth-life was wrapped around me ...
the hour I lived through wakefully

                    in Saturn's rays of many-coloured light.
                    Through my earthly thinking,
                    this spiritual experience has been kept shrouded
                        from me
                    in the darkness of my soul.
                    It rises now into the light!

ASTRID   In cosmic light you spoke these words:
                    'Eternal time, hear this my ardent prayer—
                    flow mightily into this blessedness;
                    and let the teacher, let the other soul,
                    abide with me within you, filled with peace.'

MARIA   And may you, present moment, abide with me as
                        well—
                    you who could create for me this spiritual event
                    as a power in myself. Strengthen me,
                    that from my soul you do not vanish like a dream.
                    Within the light that shines at the midnight hour—
                    the light that Astrid forms for me out of the darkness
                        of my soul—
                    my ego now unites unto that Self
                    who created me to be its servant in the world.
                    But how can I maintain this present moment,
                    that when I sense earth's brightness round about me
                        once again
                    I do not lose it?
                    For the senses' power is great,
                    and if it works to deaden what has been seen in
                        spirit,
                    then dead this may remain,
                    when to the spirit the self returns.

                    (Luna appears as if summoned by these last words.)

LUNA   This present moment could create for you a power
                        of will.
                    Safeguard it now,
                    before sense-existence makes you dream again.
                    Recall the words that at the midnight hour

	I spoke to you.
MARIA	Luna, from the cosmic midnight hour, you've brought the power of will to me, which shall support my earthly life.
LUNA	And from my words there followed the Guardian's warning: 'When now you stand before yourself in spirit, you'll see yourself in ancient times transformed. You'll learn how wings for spiritual ascent are strengthened also if the soul should fall. The wish to fall should never tempt the soul; but from each fall it must acquire new wisdom.'
MARIA	The power of your words ... where is it leading me? A spirit-star ... there on the shores of soul. It shines ... approaching me ... as spirit-form. With my own Self it comes ... As it draws near its light condenses. Forms are darkening in the light ... They are becoming living beings ... A young neophyte ... a sacrificial flame ... the strict command of the Chief Hierophant to read aright the Word within the flame. The priests around ... confused and terrified by this young neophyte's confession ...

(The Guardian of the Threshold appears during these last words.)

GUARDIAN	And now in spirit-hearing understand the strict command of the Chief Hierophant.
MARIA	'Then read, O human soul, what from the flame in cosmic Word your inmost core proclaims.' Who spoke these words, which my own thought recalls and bears to me from flowing tides of soul?

(Benedictus appears during Maria's words.)

BENEDICTUS With my own words you've summoned me.
When long ago I gave you that command,
you were not ready then to follow me.
My words, however, rested in the womb of world-events.
There, in the course of time, they gathered strength,
which from your own soul's life flowed out to them.
And so, during your later lives on earth,
they worked on unconsciously within your depths of soul.
Through them, you could find me once again as teacher.
They rise now into conscious thought
and are transformed into a potent meaning for your life.
'The sacrificial work that we fulfil
is of significance not for ourselves alone:
within our sacred act, world-destiny
streams as a mighty force through word and deed.'

MARIA It was not you who spoke these words;
it was the Hierophant who assisted you
in that ancient Temple-brotherhood.
He knew that powers of destiny had already foreordained
the ending of this brotherhood.
He sensed the shining dawn of beauty's splendour,
which heralded a new sun rising over Hellas
within the spiritual life of earth.
And so he did not send into my soul
those thoughts whose power should have worked on me.
During the course of that initiation,
he felt the pulse of cosmic evolution
and so could serve as instrument of the gods.
One thing he spoke, wrenched from his deepest soul:
'Loneliness—here in this solemn and sacred place,

	I have come to know you deeply.
	Why am I alone here?'

BENEDICTUS And so the seed of solitude was planted in his soul.
In the womb of time it ripened and bore fruit.
In turning towards mysticism, Capesius is now
    tasting this fruit.
And it is driving him to follow Felix's example.

MARIA But there is still that woman, lingering in the
    precincts of the Temple.
Although I saw her as she was in ancient times,
I cannot yet perceive her in her present form.
How will I be able to find her
when sense-existence makes me dream again?

GUARDIAN You'll find her when in realms of soul
you see the being that she herself is sensing
as shade among the shades.
With all the power of her soul
she is pursuing it.
She will only be able to set it free
from its spell-bound state in the realm of shades,
when in her present form she can behold through
    you
her long-past life on earth.

(The Guardian of the Threshold and Benedictus disappear.)

MARIA There, as a shining star of soul—
the solemn Guardian.
He moves towards the shoreline of my soul.
Far and wide his shining spreads tranquillity.
He radiates a power sublime
and his solemnity sends strength into my deepest
    being.
I will submerge myself in his tranquillity,
for I can feel how through it I'll be able
to raise myself to full awakening of spirit.

And you, my faithful messengers of soul,
as shining stars I'll keep you close to me.
Astrid—you I'll call upon,
when thoughts would lose their light-filled clarity.
And Luna—may my word find you,
when in the depths my power of will is sleeping.

(Curtain.)

SCENE 10

The same room as in the preceding scene. Johannes alone in meditation.

JOHANNES   'This is the hour in which he offers up his being
to age-old service in the Mysteries ...
Perhaps the revelation of a dream
will let me linger with him yet awhile in spirit.'

These are the words that woman spoke ...
in ancient times ... within the precincts of the
    Temple ...
I see her as an image formed in spirit,
and holding her in thought,
I feel that I myself grow stronger.
What is it that this image stirs in me?
And why am I held so riveted by it?
It's not that I am drawn to it through any power of
    sympathy,
for if I were to see it in the senses' world,
I would be quite unmoved by it.
What is it trying to say to me?

OTHER PHILIA *(voice from the distance)*
'The enchanted weaving
of their own inmost being.'

JOHANNES   'And wakening-dreaming
to souls is revealing
the enchanted weaving
of their own inmost being.'

(While Johannes is speaking, the Other Philia approaches.)

Mysterious spirit, who are you?
You gave to me true counsel,

> but at the same time you deceived me about
> yourself.

OTHER PHILIA
> Johannes, out of yourself you have created
> the double-form of your own being.
> I too must circle round you as a shade,
> until that time when you yourself set free
> the Shadow who, through your guilt,
> is forced to lead a spell-bound life.

JOHANNES This is the third time you speak these words to me.
> I will be led by them. Show me the way.

OTHER PHILIA
> Johannes, what has been preserved for you within
> yourself—
> seek for it now, alive in spirit light.
> From its own light it will give light to you.
> You will be able then to see
> how in a later life you'll expiate your guilt.

JOHANNES *How* can I seek for what within myself
> has been preserved for me, alive in spirit light?

OTHER PHILIA
> Give me what you are in thinking
> and lose yourself a little while in me.
> But do not change into another being.

JOHANNES How shall I give myself to you
> before I have seen you in your true being?

OTHER PHILIA
> I am within you—part of your own soul.
> I am the living power of love in you,
> the hope that stirs within your heart,
> the fruits of long-past lives on earth
> preserved for you within your being—
> behold them now through me.

                    Feel what I am in you;
                    and through my power within you, see yourself!
                    Then understand the meaning of that image,
                    which you perceived without sympathy.

                    (The Other Philia disappears.)

JOHANNES   Mysterious spirit, I can feel you within me,
                and yet I can no longer see you.
                Where are you then?

OTHER PHILIA *(voice from the distance)*
                    'The enchanted weaving
                    of their own inmost being.'

JOHANNES   'The enchanted weaving
                of their own inmost being.'
                You enchanted weaving of my own inmost being,
                teach me the meaning of that image,
                which I perceived without sympathy.

                The power of these words—where is it leading me?
                A spirit-star ... there on the shores of soul;
                it shines ... approaching me as spirit-form.
                As it draws near its light grows ever brighter;
                and forms are taking shape as living beings.

                A young neophyte ... a sacrificial flame ...
                the strict command of the Chief Hierophant
                to read aright the Word within the flame ...

                The woman seeks for the young neophyte—
                the woman I perceived without sympathy.

                (Maria appears as a thought-form of Johannes.)

MARIA   Before the sacred flame, who thought of you?
                Who felt you near the place of sacrifice?
                Johannes, if from enchanted worlds of soul
                you would set free your shadow-being,

then *live* the aims that shine on you from him.
The path that you are following will lead you on,
but first you must rediscover it aright.
That woman in the precincts of the Temple
will show it to you,
when she can strongly live within your thinking.
Enchanted in the realm of shades,
she is pursuing the shadow-being,
who now through you is forced to serve
the aims of cruel, unfeeling shadows.

(The Spirit of Johannes' Youth appears.)

SPIRIT OF JOHANNES' YOUTH

    I shall remain forever bound to you,
if lovingly you tend those powers
preserved for me within the womb of time
by that young neophyte whom in ages past
your soul was seeking at the place of sacrifice.
But you must also truly see the one
at whose side I now appear to you.

MARIA

    Maria, in the form you wished to see her,
does not exist in worlds where truth prevails.
My sacred vow is radiating strength,
that you hold fast to what you have achieved.
You find me in the shining fields of light,
where beauty creates powers of life.
Now seek me in the deepest ground of worlds,
where souls win back their feeling for the gods
through Love which in all worlds perceives the Self.

(During Maria's last lines, Lucifer appears.)

LUCIFER

    Compelling powers, work!
And feel, you elemental beings,
the power of your master.
Make smooth the path,
so that what my wish craves,
what follows my will,

can turn from realms of earth
to Lucifer's domain.

(Benedictus appears.)

BENEDICTUS   Maria's sacred vow is radiating strength.
It streams into his soul a healing light.
He will admire you,
but he will not succumb to you.

LUCIFER   I will give battle!

BENEDICTUS   And battling serve the gods!

(Curtain.)

SCENE 11

The same room as in the two preceding scenes. Benedictus and Strader enter.

STRADER You spoke grave words ... and Maria too ...
such harsh and cutting words,
when you both appeared to me at my life's abyss.

BENEDICTUS You know it's not the images in themselves that are important.
They're but the revelation of an inner content
seeking to enter the soul.

STRADER But what they had to say to me was hard to bear:
'Where is your light? You are radiating darkness.
Into the light you work chaotic darkness.'
And so these words, which I took to be Maria's,
were actually a revelation of the Spirit.

BENEDICTUS Since you had progressed one stage higher on your spiritual path,
the Spirit which had raised you up
showed you the level you were at before as darkness.
It came to you in the form of Maria,
because this is how your own soul pictured it.
My dear Strader, the Spirit is now working strongly in you;
and you are being swiftly led to higher levels on the Path.

STRADER But even so, what I heard was terrible:
'You are too cowardly to radiate your light.'
The Spirit spoke these words to me as well.

BENEDICTUS The Spirit *had* to call you cowardly,
because what for less developed souls is bravery

is indeed cowardice for you.
As we progress, what once was courage becomes cowardice
which must be overcome.

STRADER
These words ... they touch me deeply.
Just recently, Romanus told me of his plan:
if I were to agree to carry out the work without your help,
then he'd be prepared to stand by Hilary
with all his earthly means and influence.
When I objected to this, and told him
that I'd never separate my work from you and your circle,
he replied that in that case all further effort was in vain.
In taking such a stance,
Romanus is supporting the Manager in his opposition to our plans.
And without these plans,
my whole life appears to me completely futile.
Since these two men have ripped away from me my field of action,
I can see nothing at all in front of me
but a life ... bereft of *life*.
In order that my spirit is not lamed by this,
I need that courage of which you spoke just now.
But whether I shall prove strong enough in this,
I cannot tell.
For I feel how the very power that I am struggling to liberate
at the same time turns against me destructively.

BENEDICTUS
Maria and Johannes have recently progressed in spiritual vision.
Nothing now is stopping them from working out of life in spirit-realms
into sense-existence.
In the course of time, new aims will be found
uniting you with them.

'What must *will* be.'
These occult words have value not as a *teaching*,
but as a source of creative strength.
Let us then wait
and watch for the signs the Spirit will give to us.

STRADER Just recently an image came to me
which I took to be a sign of destiny.
I was aboard a ship; you were at the helm.
My job was to attend to the working of the rudder.
We were taking Maria and Johannes to the place
where they were to start their work.
Then another ship appeared alongside ours;
aboard it were Romanus and the Manager.
They launched an attack on us. I fought against
    them.
Suddenly, Ahriman entered the battle, fighting on
    their side.
I saw myself in fierce combat with him.
Then Theodora came to my aid;
and after that the image vanished from my sight.
I once told Capesius and Felix
that I could easily bear the opposition,
which from the outer world is now threatening my
    work;
yes, even if it were to shatter all my hopes,
I would be able to endure it.
And now I'm thinking ... perhaps this image is
    telling me
that outer opposition is the expression of an *inner*
    battle—
a battle against Ahriman?
If so, am I ready for this battle?

BENEDICTUS My friend, I see this image has not yet fully matured
    for you.
I feel you'll be able to increase the power by which it
    came to you.
I also feel that if you can strengthen yourself
    sufficiently

> you'll win new forces, both for yourself and for your friends.
> This much I can sense; but *how* it will come to pass I cannot see.

(Curtain.)

SCENE 12

The interior of the earth. Gigantic crystalline forms, with streams like lava breaking through them. The whole scene dully lit, in part transparent and in part translucent. Red flames above, as if compressed from the roof downwards.

AHRIMAN The stuff of being is falling from above;
I must make use of it.
Within this realm of form,
demonic matter seeps away.
A man is striving to obliterate from his being
all traces of the spiritual substance he received from
    me.
Till now I've managed to inspire him—just about!
But he's got far too close to that bunch of mystics,
who, through the guidance of Benedictus,
have achieved awakening at the midnight hour.
Lucifer has lost his hold on them;
Maria and Johannes have escaped his realm of light.
I must maintain my grip on Strader.
If I have *him*, I've got the others too.
Johannes has already blunted himself badly on my
    shadow;
he knows me well.
I cannot get at him except through Strader.
And with Maria—it is just the same.
But maybe Strader won't yet be able
to see through all that spiritual confusion
which human beings call Nature.
He'll fail to see it for what it really is—
just so much spirit-baggage left lying around by me.
He'll presuppose the blind working of energy and
    matter
there where I—denying spirit—spiritually create.
Admittedly, the others have blabbered on to him for
    hours

about the nature of my being and realm.
And yet, I don't consider him completely lost.
He'll forget that with his half-baked knowledge
he was sent to me by Benedictus
to be exorcised of the belief
that I am just a fabrication of the human brain.
However, if at the right time I am to get a hold on him,
I'll need some earthly help.
I'll call down a human soul—
one who thinks himself so very clever
that for him I am nothing but a fraud
invented for the benefit of idiots.
He serves me now and then, when I have need of him.

(Ahriman goes out and returns with Ferdinand Reinecke's soul, which appears as a kind of copy of Ahriman himself. He removes a blindfold from Ferdinand Reinecke's eyes.)

He must leave his earthly reason at the door.
He should not *understand* what he'll experience here.
For he is still an honest soul
and would do nothing for me, if he understood
what lies behind the impulses I'll now inspire into him.
All that transpires here he later must forget.

Do you know Dr Strader—my servant?

FERDINAND REINECKE'S SOUL

He struts about up there on that earth-star.
Out of his learned drivel, he attempts
to build up structures that can stand in life—
but every puff of *real* life blows them down.
He greedily laps up anything those mystic windbags care to utter.
He's already almost suffocating in their fumes.

> And now he's trying to spread his fog around Hilary
>   as well,
> whose Manager, however, keeps him well in check,
> because otherwise that bunch of lying toads
> would utterly destroy the reputation of his firm
> with all their spiritual hogwash.

AHRIMAN
> Such prattle will get us nowhere!
> *Strader* is the man I need.
> So long as he can maintain faith in himself,
> it will be far too easy for Benedictus to succeed
> in bringing out his teaching to humanity.
> The Manager may well be serving *Lucifer*—
> I've got to go about things differently.
> Through Strader I must damage Benedictus.
> For Benedictus and his other pupils
> will achieve nothing without Strader.
> Admittedly, my opponents still have the upper
>   hand.
> When Strader dies, they'll have him for themselves.
> But if, whilst he is still alive on earth,
> I manage to confuse his soul
> and make him doubt himself,
> then Benedictus will no longer be able
> to use him as the frontman of his campaign.
> From the Book of Destiny it is already known to me
> that Strader's life will soon come to its end.
> This Benedictus cannot see.
>
> My loyal servant, you are almost super-clever.
> You think that I am nothing but a childish
>   invention.
> Your reasoning is so astute
> that people are impelled to listen to you.
> Go straight to Strader. Prove to him
> that his machine contains a flaw.
> Convince him that the reason it will not work
> is not the unfavourability of the times,
> but the fact that it's been ill-conceived.

FERDINAND REINECKE'S SOUL
For that I have been well prepared.
For a long time, all my faculties have been directed
   to this one aim—
how best to prove to Strader that he has gone astray.
If someone has for years, through many a sleepless
   night,
racked his brains thinking about such stuff,
then it's easy for him to believe
that the reason for the failure of his invention
does not lie in his own thinking
but in some external factor.
In Strader's case, it's really quite pathetic.
If he hadn't befogged his mind with mysticism,
and relied instead on common-sense and intellect,
then humanity would certainly have reaped great
   benefits
from his considerable gifts.

AHRIMAN
Arm yourself now with all your cleverness.
Your task is to make Strader lose all confidence in
   himself.
If you succeed in this,
he'll no longer want to stick by Benedictus,
who will in turn be thrown back on himself
and his *own* teachings.
And *these* are unpalatable to human beings;
the more they are revealed in their true form,
the more they will be hated on the earth.

FERDINAND REINECKE'S SOUL
I see it now; it's crystal clear.
I know how I will demonstrate to Strader
the errors of his thinking:
his invention has a fundamental flaw,
which he cannot see
because his involvement with the mystics
is darkening his sight.
With my more sober mind,
I'll be of far better service to him.

For a long time now I've wanted this,
but I've never known just how to go about it.
Now, at last, I feel I am *inspired!*
I must consider all the details very carefully,
in order to convince Dr Strader of the truth.

(Ahriman, after replacing the blindfold, leads out the soul of Ferdinand Reinecke.)

AHRIMAN   He'll serve me well.
The flame of spiritual knowledge being kindled on
    the earth
is burning me.
I must go on working there,
without allowing the mystics to expose my working
    to the world.

(Theodora's soul appears.)

THEODORA'S SOUL
Though you may assail Strader with all your
    strength,
you will find *me* at his side.
Because he came to me on light-filled paths of soul,
he is united to me—
both on earth and in the realms of spirit.

AHRIMAN   If she really will not leave his side
while he is still alive on earth,
the battle will be lost for me.
But I have not yet given up hope
that in the end he will forget her.

(Curtain.)

SCENE 13

A large reception room in Hilary's house. Hilary in conversation with Romanus.

HILARY
It's painful to have to admit to you
that the knot of destiny which has been formed
　　within our circle
is almost crushing me.
What is there to build upon
when all around us everything is threatening to
　　collapse?
Through you, the friends of Benedictus
have been excluded from what we're trying to do.
And now Strader is being tormented by the agonies
　　of doubt.
A certain man, who has often opposed our efforts in
　　the past
with great cleverness ... and hatred too ...
has been able to prove to him
that his invention has been fundamentally
　　misconceived—
that the problem lies with the machine itself,
and not in any external constraint.
My life has been in vain. I wanted deeds;
but I always lacked the ideas to bring them into
　　being.
This barrenness of soul has tormented me most
　　bitterly.
The only thing that has always sustained me
has been my spiritual vision.
Yet even this ... in Strader's case ... deceived me.

ROMANUS
I've often had a nightmarish feeling of oppression,
when I observed how in the course of events
your words were shown to be seriously mistaken,

and your spiritual vision, therefore, seemed to be
 deceiving you.
This experience became for me a source of inner
 guidance.
It was gradually transformed into a feeling
on which I can base my judgement now:
you've trusted too blindly in your spiritual vision,
and so it can now appear to be deceiving you
when actually it's leading you to the truth.
In the case of Strader you have seen correctly,
in spite of everything that clever man has proved.

HILARY So you've not lost faith?
You still believe in Strader?

ROMANUS My faith in him had nothing whatsoever to do with
 his friends.
And it will remain unchanged,
regardless of whether his invention succeeds or fails.
If he *was* mistaken—well, what of it?
It's only through error that we find the truth.

HILARY You mean, the failure of his invention doesn't
 trouble you—
you, to whom life has brought nothing but success?

ROMANUS Success comes when one is not afraid to fail.
We should understand this particular case
in the light of spiritual knowledge.
Then we shall see quite clearly how things stand
 with Strader.
He'll most certainly prove victorious in the battle,
opening for him the gates into the spiritual world.
Undaunted he will pass the Guardian
who stands before the threshold of that world.
For some time, I have carried in my heart
the word of that stern Guardian.
I sense his presence now at Strader's side.
Whether *Strader* is perceiving him,
or is approaching him unconsciously,

| | I cannot know for sure.
But I believe I know him well enough to say
that with great courage he will realize the truth
that self-knowledge must cause pain:
'In one who bravely yields to the unknown,
there shall arise new inner powers of will;
and strengthened by the living springs of hope,
he'll bear the pain which his self-knowledge brings.' |

HILARY My friend, thank you for these occult words.
Although I've often heard them spoken in the past,
it is only now that in my *heart*
I fully understand their hidden meaning.
The cosmic ways are hard to understand.
And I must wait ...
until the Spirit points to me the way
in keeping with my vision.

(Hilary and Romanus exit stage-left. Capesius and Felix Balde, led in by the Secretary, enter from stage-right.)

SECRETARY I expected Benedictus to return from his journey today,
but I'm afraid he's not yet back.
If you'll try again tomorrow,
I'm sure you'll be able to see him.

FELIX BALDE Then would it be possible for us to speak with Hilary?

SECRETARY I'll tell him that you're here.

(Exit Secretary.)

FELIX BALDE What you experienced is certainly of great significance.
Would you mind relating it to me again?
These things can only be evaluated properly
when one has fully grasped them in the spirit.

CAPESIUS	It was just this morning; I felt the mystic mood approaching me—
	the senses silent ... memory stilled as well ...
	in expectation of a spiritual event.
	It came ... to begin with just as is now well known to me.
	But then, quite distinctly, there appeared the soul of Strader.
	At first he did not speak,
	and I had time to check my degree of wakefulness.
	But then I heard him say these words quite clearly:
	'Do not depart from the true mystic mood.'
	They seemed to come from the depths of his soul.
	And he continued most emphatically:
	'To strive for nothing ...
	to rest in complete peacefulness of soul ...
	one's inmost being in a state of pure expectation—
	this is the mystic mood. And it awakens of itself,
	quite unsought within the stream of life,
	when the human soul has strengthened itself rightly,
	and when, through powers of thought, it seeks the spirit actively.
	This mood may come more often in our quiet hours,
	but it can also come in the thick of action.
	For this to happen, it is only necessary
	that the soul's more subtle inner vision of the spirit
	is not thoughtlessly abandoned.'
FELIX BALDE	An echo of my own words ... though somewhat changed ...
CAPESIUS	Examined more carefully,
	they could appear to mean the exact *opposite* of your words!
	And one is led even closer to this conclusion
	when one considers what he went on to say:
	'But when the mystic mood is *artificially* awakened,
	then one's inner being is led only into *itself*;
	and like a curtain, the darkness of one's personal life of soul

	is drawn across the light. And if you try to do this out of *mysticism*, then with mystical delusions you'll destroy your spirit sight.'
FELIX BALDE	This can be nothing other than my own words turned round through Strader's way of thinking and repeated now in you as a serious spiritual error.
CAPESIUS	And Strader's final words were these: 'The spiritual world will remain forever closed to one who tries to enter it through *seeking*. And truth does not reside within the soul of one who has for many years *sought but a mood*.'

(Philia appears, visible only to Capesius. Felix Balde shows by his bearing that he does not comprehend the following.)

PHILIA	Capesius, if soon you will pay heed to what is shown to you unsought in seeking, the many-coloured light will strengthen you, and fill you through and through with living images. The forces of your soul reveal this light to you. What radiates from your own sun-filled being Saturn's ripened wisdom will subdue. And to your inner eye will be revealed what you as earthly human being can comprehend. Then I myself will lead you to the Guardian, who stands before the Threshold of the Spirit.
FELIX BALDE	From spheres unknown to me there sound forth words; and yet their tones create no bright existence. And so they are not fully real to me.
CAPESIUS	The guidance Philia now gives to me will lead me on, that there may come a time when what I can already comprehend

in my own life as human being on earth
shall be revealed to me in spirit too.

(Curtain.)

SCENE 14

The same room as in the preceding scene. Hilary's wife in conversation with the Manager.

HILARY'S WIFE
    It almost seems that destiny itself opposes the initiative
    which my husband believed so vital for the world;
    for think how tangled are the threads of all our lives
    which have been so tightly tied together in this knot.

MANAGER A knot of destiny, which at the present time
    seems to human powers of reasoning quite impossible to untie . . .
    and therefore must be cut.
    I see no other possibility:
    your husband and I must go our separate ways.

HILARY'S WIFE
    My husband would never want to separate from you.
    It completely contradicts the spirit of the firm—
    that spirit carried over from his dear father,
    and loyally continued by the son.

MANAGER But hasn't this loyalty already been betrayed?
    The goals that Hilary has been setting for himself
    quite certainly divert him from the path
    his father always tried to follow.

HILARY'S WIFE
    My husband's happiness in life
    depends now completely on the attainment of those goals.
    Ever since they were first conceived by him—
    flashing up like lightning in his mind—

I've seen how he has been transformed.
Life had become for him empty and barren.
He took great pains to conceal this, even from his
	closest friends,
but all the more did it eat away at him from within.
He felt his life was worthless,
for he never had any ideas
that seemed to him to be of value to the world.
Then, when the idea of this project with the pupils of
	Benedictus came to him,
he was rejuvenated—a new man, fulfilled and
	happy.
And for the first time he felt he was doing something
	worthwhile with his life.
It was simply unthinkable to him that you could ever
	oppose his plans ...
until it happened.
Then it came as a crushing blow
like he'd never experienced in his life before.
If you only knew what he has suffered through your
	opposition,
you'd certainly soften the hard line you are taking.

MANAGER   To go against my own convictions
would be like throwing away my human dignity.
Working alongside Strader was not going to be easy
	for me.
But I decided I would take this on
and lend my support to your husband's scheme,
because *Romanus* was behind it;
and with *him* I've been able to see eye to eye
ever since he spoke to me of Strader.
What he then said to me
marked the starting-point of my own path of
	spiritual development.
There was a power in his words
that streamed into my soul and worked on me.
It was a thing I'd never felt before.
And even if I cannot fully understand the words he
	spoke,

they must surely be of deep significance to me.
It is only Strader whom Romanus supports.
In his opinion, the contribution of the others
would not only hinder the work—
it would also be a danger to themselves.
I have such a high regard for Romanus' opinion
that I am now convinced
that if Strader cannot find the way to engage his will
   without his friends,
he would have to take this as a sign of destiny—
a sign that for the time being he should remain with
   his friends,
and only *later* create out of his own striving
the impulses for deeds in outer life.
The fact that he has recently become much closer to
   these friends of his,
after having been estranged from them for a while,
leads me to believe that he will be able to adapt,
even if for the moment it might seem to him
that his goals have all been swept away.

HILARY'S WIFE

You are only seeing him through Romanus' eyes.
You should try to look at him more objectively.
He can devote himself to spiritual life so completely
that he appears at times quite distant from the earth.
The spirit is then fully present to him.
And Theodora is for him at these times still alive—
you can feel her presence when you speak to him.
There are many who are able to speak about the
   spirit
in such a way that on later reflection their words
   impress one with their truth.
What *Strader* has to say works in the spoken word
   itself.
It's clear how little he values merely subjective
   spiritual experience
that is content to remain at the level of feeling—
how it is always the urge for objective spiritual
   research that leads him.

And in this way he doesn't allow his spiritual striving
to confuse a scientific and practical mind.
Try to see this side of him, and you will realize
that you should value his own judgement of his
   friends
more highly than the one which you've been given
by Romanus.

MANAGER In this matter, which lies well outside my
   accustomed field of thought,
Romanus' judgement is the only solid ground on
   which I can stand.
If I really were to enter into the realm of spiritual
   knowledge,
I would need such guidance as could only be given
   to me
by someone who has gained my complete trust—
someone whom I could completely understand.

(The Secretary enters.)

You look disturbed. What's happened?

SECRETARY *(hesitantly)*
A few hours ago Dr Strader died.

MANAGER Dead ... Strader?

HILARY'S WIFE
Dr Strader dead!
Where's Hilary?

SECRETARY He's in his room ... as if paralysed by the news ...
It was brought to him just now from Strader's
   house.

(Hilary's wife goes out, followed by the Secretary.)

MANAGER *(alone)*
Strader dead ... Is this reality?

Am I already now being touched by that spiritual
   sleep
of which I've heard so much? . . .
How dark the face of destiny which here directs our
   lives . . .

O little soul of mine, what mighty power
has taken hold of your life now
and made it part of this great knot of destiny?

What must be *will* be!

Why is it that these words have never left me,
ever since that time when Strader spoke them to
   Hilary and myself?
They sounded then as if they were coming to him
   from another world . . .
as if he was inspired by the spirit!

So what is it that *must* be?

I feel how I was taken hold of by the spirit at that
   time,
and in those words I hear it speaking to me now—
a strange and solemn language . . .

How can I learn to understand it?

(Curtain.)

SCENE 15

The same room as in the two preceding scenes. Strader's nurse is seated, waiting. The Secretary enters.

SECRETARY Benedictus will presently be here
to receive the message from you personally.
He's just returned from his journey.

He was a great man, Dr Strader.
At first I had little faith in Hilary's grand ideas.
But because I was often present when Strader was describing to him
exactly what was required for the work,
I soon lost all my earlier objections.
Always with great enthusiasm and energy,
and with the keenest sense for everything that is both possible and attainable,
he strove to realize his final goal in close conformity with the facts,
taking pains to avoid all groundless speculation.
His conduct was always in keeping with the ways of the true mystic—
like one who, wishing to see the beauty of a distant landscape from a mountain-top,
waits till he has reached the summit,
and does not form a mental-picture of it in advance.

NURSE *You* knew him in the midst of his activities,
standing fully in the stream of life—
a man of great gifts, a mighty spirit.
In the short time it was granted me
to nurse him in his last days on the earth,
I was able to recognize the greatness of his *soul*—
this gentle soul, who, except for seven rare years of happiness,
had always gone his way through life alone.

	His colleagues offered him their wisdom.
	But it was *love* he needed.
	Indeed, his yearning to be active in the world *was* love—
	the love that shows itself in life in so many different ways.
	What this soul sought through spiritual knowledge was as necessary to the noble fire of his being as sleep is to the body after labour.
SECRETARY	And yet spiritual knowledge was for him also the *source* of all his work.
	In the most beautiful way, it permeated everything he did completely ...
NURSE	... because it was his nature always to love and to unite his soul with everything life brought to him.
	His last thoughts were about his work to which he'd been so lovingly devoted.
	Like one departing from a beloved friend, Strader's soul took leave of his earthly work.
SECRETARY	Like a true mystic soul he was able to live fully in the spirit.
	And Theodora was always present to him, as though she were living still ...
NURSE	... because his loneliness united him to her.
	She was with him when he died.
	He felt as though he were being called by her to bring his work to its fulfilment in the spiritual world.
	A few hours before he died he wrote these words for Benedictus, which I shall presently pass on to him.
	And so we must continue on this earth, our lives so dark with riddles, yet lit up by sun-filled souls amidst us such as he,

from whom, like planets circling, we receive
the light that can awaken powers of life.

(Benedictus enters; the Secretary leaves.)

Before his last strength failed him,
Strader was still able to write down these few lines.
I give them now to you, his friend in spirit.

BENEDICTUS   And when he'd written down these words,
what was it that was occupying him at the end?

NURSE   At first his thoughts were with his latest project.
And then in spirit Theodora joined him.
Feeling this, his soul was gently released from its
   earthly body.

BENEDICTUS   I thank you, faithful soul, for these last services,
which you were able still to give him on the earth.

(The Nurse goes out. Benedictus reads Strader's words.)

'My friend, when I learnt that the obstruction to my
   work
arose not only from external sources
but through defects within its basic conception,
I was almost completely crushed.
And then there came to me again
that image which I recently described to you.
But this time it ended differently.
It was not Ahriman who rose up against me as my
   opponent;
it was a spirit-messenger, whose form vividly
   appeared to me
as the embodiment of my own faulty thinking.
I remembered then the words you spoke to me
about the strengthening of my inner being;
and immediately ... the figure vanished.'

There are a few more words ... I cannot read them.

> A chaos, weaving a dark veil of thought,
> is working to conceal them from me now.
>
> *(Ahriman appears; Benedictus sees him.)*
>
> Who are you, who out of my chaos
> comes to life within my soul's horizon ... like a shadow.

AHRIMAN *(to himself)*
> He sees me, but he does not recognize me.
> And so he will not yet cause me pain,
> if I attempt to work now at his side.
>
> *(To Benedictus.)*
>
> I can reveal to you more fully
> what Strader wishes to confide in you—
> for your own benefit
> and for the spiritual progress of your pupils too.

BENEDICTUS
> My circle of friends will always know itself
> to be connected with the soul of Strader,
> even though the senses can no longer be our bridge to him.
> But should a spirit-messenger approach us,
> claiming to be sent from Strader's worlds,
> he first must win our trust
> by revealing himself to our spiritual vision,
> so that he can be fully known to us.

AHRIMAN
> But you are seeking for *self*-knowledge, are you not?
> And therefore, any unknown spirit-entity wishing to do you service,
> would have to show itself as *part of your own self*,
> before it could be fully *known* to you.

BENEDICTUS
> Whoever you may be, you only serve the good,
> when your striving is not directed towards yourself,

but when, instead, you lose yourself in human
   thinking,
and thereby are reborn within the world's evolving.

AHRIMAN   It's time that I took leave of him—and quickly too.
For when his vision can *conceive* me as in truth I am,
then there will be formed within his thinking
a part of that power which slowly will destroy me.

(Ahriman disappears.)

BENEDICTUS   Only now do I recognize Ahriman.
He flees from here, yet not without creating in me
knowledge of his being.
He attempts to deceive human thinking,
because, following an ancient error,
he sees in it the source of all his pain.
He has not yet realized
that in the future he will only be redeemed
when he can find himself again reflected in this
   thinking.
And so, although he does indeed reveal himself to
   human beings,
it is never as in truth he really is.
Revealing himself, yet at the same time remaining
   cunningly concealed,
he tried in Strader's case to seize the moment,
seeking through him to exert an influence on his
   friends as well.

But in the future, he will not be able to disguise his
   being
from the circle of my pupils.
In inner wakefulness, they shall be able to conceive
   him
when he attempts to work within their spiritual
   vision.
They shall discern the many forms in which he tries
   to hide
when he reveals himself to human souls.

But you, sun-ripened soul of Strader
who, through the strengthening of your spiritual
  powers,
have compelled the messenger of error to take
  flight—
you shall become a spirit-star to lighten our friends'
  paths;
you shall in future ever shine your light upon Maria
  and Johannes,
that, through you, they may find the power they
  need
to arm themselves more strongly for their work,
and, as revealers of the inner light,
prove steadfast in their thought, even at those times,
when over clear and wakeful spirit-vision,
Ahriman, opposing human wisdom,
would spread his dark and gloomy night of chaos.

(Curtain.)

A NOTE ON THE TRANSLATION

Rudolf Steiner wrote almost all of the lines of his four mystery dramas in a regular iambic pentameter rhythm. One of our major stylistic deviations from the original has been to break with this in all but three scenes. Especially where the content was of events in the physical world, we found that this regular rhythm was, as T.S. Eliot discovered when he came to write verse drama, 'too remote from the movement of modern speech' for it to convey the impression of conversation. We tried instead a free verse form that employs continual variation in rhythm and length of line. This gave us many possibilities of style. We could be poetic and avoid a naturalism of speaking, and yet also give the impression of down-to-earth dramatic encounter when this was required.

Businessmen in conversation in an office, an artist lapsing into a lyrical reverie in the midst of Nature, the language of the elemental forces of Nature (gnomes & sylphs), the resolves of human souls in the spiritual world before their birth, the mantric words of an initiation ceremony in ancient Egypt ... these are some of the dramatic situations in this play for which we have tried to find an appropriate style of language. The right style is not created by employing literary devices, but, in the words of David Wansborough, results from being able to 'recreate the gesture of events by employing forms that use a meter or speech rhythm evoked by the changes in the breath stream when events are relived' (*A Pillar of Salt?*, 1988). On the quest for this ever-varying style, we found we *did* go back to the iambic pentameter rhythm in certain places—for both the scenes set in the spiritual world (scenes 5 and 6) and for the Egyptian initiation ceremony (scene 8). This rhythm seemed in the former case to serve the purpose of lifting the content of these purely spiritual scenes as far as possible away from the level of day-to-day reality, while in the latter the very strictness of the rhythm lent itself to the mantric, ceremonial language of the scene, and helped to evoke the quality of that austere time and situation. We have also been as strict as possible when following particular rhythms employed by Steiner—for example with the words of the gnomes and sylphs and some of the mantric words of the soul-forces. And dotted throughout the text are passages of regular iambic pentameter where the content needed lifting due to its significance.

In places, it might be felt that our translation has not yet been thoroughly received into the English language. We might at times have liked to simplify and get the general meaning across in a more comfortable English form—but we have always seen ourselves as translators, not free-renderers. Steiner's thought-structures are extremely subtle and complex and put great strain on the English language. Yet we also found that English demands a more down-to-earth formulation, so that for passages which are somewhat ambiguous in the original German (even for native-speakers) we were forced to make some definite decisions with regard to the meaning.

It should be mentioned that the title of the play, if literally translated, would be *The Souls' Awakening*. This is a shortening by Steiner himself of an earlier version: *Johannes' and Maria's Souls' Awakening*. In our version we have used the term 'soul' in its general form in order to avoid raising the question: 'Whose souls?', and to give the title a more universal ring. Our title is, therefore, a shortening of the full title in the form: *The Soul's Awaking of Johannes and Maria*.

It should also be mentioned that our stage-directions are in the English form—i.e. from the actor's point of view, where stage-left, for example, is the right side of the stage as seen by the audience.

M.B., A.L.